THE
JOHN WESLEY
TREASURY

THE
JOHN WESLEY TREASURY

Erwin Paul Rudolph, Editor

While this book is designed for the reader's personal enjoyment and profit, it is also intended for group study. A Leader's Guide is available from your local bookstore or from the publisher at $.75.

VICTOR BOOKS

a division of SP Publications, Inc., Wheaton, Illinois
Offices also in Fullerton, California • Whitby, Ontario, Canada • London, England

Scripture quotations are from the King James Version.

Recommended Dewey Decimal Classification: 922.7
Suggested Subject Headings: Christian Biography; Methodism;
   Sermons

Library of Congress Catalog Number: 78-66035
ISBN: 0-88207-517-9

VICTOR BOOKS
A division of SP Publications, Inc.
P.O. Box 1825 Wheaton, Ill. 60187

CONTENTS

John Wesley, the Man

Not only do historians agree that the Evangelical Revival produced permanent results, but the 20th century man still stands amazed at the achievements of John Wesley and his followers who proclaimed so powerfully the realities of the unseen and awoke the conscience of a nation from its moral lethargy.

What drove one man to travel a quarter of a million miles (mostly on horseback), to preach tens of thousands of sermons, and to cross the Irish Sea scores of times in the cause of evangelism? Whence came the power that for half a century swayed England and America, that tamed infuriated mobs, that swept aside an angered clergy, and that transformed the most degenerate into monuments of grace? Preeminently, it was the agency of the Spirit, who, brooding over the chaos of England in the 18th century, wrought this miracle. We ask, "How may lives be touched today by that same power?"

John Wesley did not grow naturally out of the soil of the 18th century, even though his long life spanned virtually all of it. His age had not recovered from the libertinism of the Restoration. Low moral standards and indifference to Christian faith characterized society. The supernatural had gone out of religious thought and practice, among a people who strove to be rational. Wesley sought to turn the church from intellectual subtleties and philosophical speculations and appealed to personal experience of the grace of God. He tolerated no scepticism from the deists, but believed in a fully inspired Bible; he recognized a Superintending Providence who protects us daily from the attacks of an indefatigable devil.

This was also the age of the aristocrat and the machine, when the middle class was rising to wealth and power. The age saw such names as Pope, Johnson, Steele, Swift, Gray, Goldsmith, and Burns in literature; Handel was composing his oratorios; Gibbon was writing *The Decline and Fall of the Roman Empire* and Adam Smith his *Wealth of Nations.* Parliament, following the Duke of Marlborough's victory at arms, was laying the foundations of the British Empire. It was during this age that God called a small, black-haired young man from Oxford University unto Himself, infused into his heart a spiritual glow, and sent him forth to shake a dying church out of its stupor.

John Wesley, born June 17, 1703, was the fifteenth child and second surviving son born to Reverend Samuel Wesley, Rector of Epworth, and his wife, Susanne. His early years were spent in Lincolnshire where his education was under the exacting direction of his mother.

His rescue from the rectory when only six years old is well known. Some malcontents set fire to his father's rectory, and when members of the family scurried to safety, John was left behind in his upstairs bedroom. As the flames leaped aloft, John's face appeared at the upstairs window. Unable to reach him, one man stood on his companion's shoulders and reached his arms up to the boy who then leaped to the arms of the rescuer as the thatched roof was collapsing. Throughout his life Wesley regarded the incident as a sign that God had spared him for a purpose. Literally and figuratively he was "a brand plucked from the burning."

After six years at Charterhouse School, he matriculated at Christ Church College, Oxford. Four years later he received the Bachelor of Arts (1726) and was elected Fellow at Lincoln's College (he had been ordained deacon in 1725). For a time he became his father's curate, visiting Oxford occasionally, where he was ordained priest in 1728. Already he was being influenced by writers who stressed deep inward piety: William Law, Jeremy Taylor, Thomas à Kempis.

Recalled from his curacy to Lincoln College, Wesley found his brother Charles associating with a small group labeled "Methodists" from their strict rules of study and religious observance. George Whitefield was among their number, and John soon became their leader.

Shortly after his father's death in 1734, Wesley embarked for Georgia to minister to the Indians, as he considered the world to be his parish. His mission there lasted less than two years, because his preaching was regarded as "too personal" and his pastoral visitation "too censorious." Brief and troubled as it was, his visit to Georgia impressed on men's minds there a new sense of spiritual reality. Wesley was beginning to sense an inner need, which had been augmented on his way to America by his association with a band of pious Moravians.

Returning to England, he sought persistently for inner spiritual assurance. He was instructed by Moravian Peter Bohler from Germany. On May 24, 1738, at Aldersgate Street, London, as a layman was reading Luther's "Preface to the Romans," Wesley received his "heartwarming experience." His life and preaching were transformed. He wrote later, "Up till then (Aldersgate), I was nearly always defeated. Now my words run like fire in stubble."

From this point Wesley became England's greatest preacher and organizer. Under the encouragement of his friend George Whitefield, when he was denied the use of Anglican pulpits, he began to preach in the open air—frequently to great throngs of people. Although he was known chiefly as an itinerant evangelist, he insisted on means of grace and fellowship of the church as essential to Christian life. He directed his efforts at first to a movement within the established church, but later he organized separate Methodist societies. For these, Wesley appointed lay leaders, with classes to nurture new Christians and remove unworthy members.

The first Methodist Conference was held in June 1744, at the Foundry, an unused commercial building purchased a few years earlier. This also became the first Methodist chapel in London. In April 1777, a short distance away—across the street from Bunhill Fields Cemetery, Wesley laid the foundation stone for the new Chapel House, which succeeded the Foundry as a place of worship. It was here that Wesley eventually died; he was buried at the rear of the chapel, March 2, 1791.

Although during half a century of his ministry he traveled some 4,500 miles each year and preached an average of twice daily, John Wesley did an immense amount of writing. In 1771-74, nearly two decades before his death, his works were collected and published in 32 volumes. On horseback, with the reins left slack, or bumping over the rough roads in a carriage, he read constantly and wrote tirelessly.

In the *Journals,* which he kept the greater part of his life and published in a series of 21 separate parts, he recorded the story of his ministry, his conduct of the affairs of the society, his journeyings, and his controversies. About the *Journal* one writer said, "We can learn better from Wesley's *Journals* than from anywhere else what manner of man Wesley was and the character of the times during which he lived."

The standard edition of Wesley's letters runs to nine volumes and contains some 2,600 letters from Wesley to all sorts and conditions of men and women. These center on the business of the Revival, on administration, pastoral problems, theological controversy, or instruction for societies or members.

Wesley preferred to be known and judged by his sermons. In them he set down simply what he found in the Bible concerning the way to heaven. Though the sermons included here are selected and abridged (as are entries from the *Letters* and *Journals*), the language is still Wesley's. What follows may accurately be called "selections from the writings." A guiding principle employed has been to provide representative sections and to delete those parts that amplify or illustrate at length the main point.

In Wesley's work we see the figure of a great preacher, an untiring worker, and a popular but autocratic leader. He reveals a mind that is shrewd, but capable of humor, and that is filled with the sense of divine mission. Simple, direct, and unpretentious, his style bears the imprint of classical scholarship.

Interestingly, some of the compliments paid to Wesley came from those outside the church he founded. Leslie Stephen described him as the greatest captain of men of his century." Even Matthew Arnold spoke of his "genius for godliness." Historian Lecky said of his spiritual crisis at Aldersgate, "It forms an epoch in English history."

The accent of Wesley's teaching was: The universality of divine grace (Christ died for all, and all who will may be saved) and the assurance of the new birth (the inner witness of the Spirit attests to this knowledge). He also emphasized the doctrine of Christian perfection (or entire sanctification), by which he meant that one must love God with all his heart, mind, soul, and strength. By doing this, no wrong temper then remained in the soul, and all one's thoughts, words, and actions were governed by pure love.

Wesley insisted that he invested no new doctrine. He said, "I simply teach the plain old religion of the Church of England." He may have built one of the world's largest denominations, but even more he put divine life into the soul of the nation. His words still lift us above worldly pursuits and direct our minds toward things eternal.

PART 1
Sermons

Salvation by Faith

"By grace are ye saved, through faith"
(Ephesians 2:8).

All the blessings which God has bestowed upon man are of His mere grace, bounty, or favor—favor altogether undeserved, man having no claim to the least of His mercies. It was free grace that "formed man of the dust of the ground, and breathed into him a living soul" and stamped on that soul the image of God and "put all things under his feet." The same free grace continues to us, at this day, life, and breath, and all things. For there is nothing we are, or have, or do which can deserve the least thing at God's hand.

Wherewithal then shall a sinful man atone for any, the least of his sins? With his own works? No. Were they ever so many or holy, they are not his own, but God's. Indeed they are all unholy and sinful themselves, so that every one of them needs a fresh atonement. Only corrupt fruit grows on a corrupt tree.

If then sinful men find favor with God, it is "grace upon grace!" If God vouchsafe still to pour fresh blessings upon us, yea, the greatest of all blessings, salvation, what can we say to these things but, "Thanks be unto God for His unspeakable gift!" And thus it is: Herein, "God commendeth His love towards us in that while we were yet sinners, Christ died" to save us. "By grace, then, are ye saved, through faith." Grace is the source, faith the condition, of salvation.

What faith is it through which we are saved? It is more than the faith of a heathen whom God requires to believe in God's existence and to give thanks for all things and to practice the moral virtues of justice, mercy, and truth towards his fellow creatures. It is more than the faith of a devil who goes farther than the heathen for he believes not only that there is a wise and powerful God, gracious to reward and just to punish, but also that Jesus is the Son of God, the Christ, the Saviour of the world. So we find him declaring in express terms, "I know Thee, who Thou art, the Holy One of God" (Luke 4:34).

Reliance on Christ

The faith through which we are saved is first a faith in Christ. It is distinguished from the faith of a heathen or devil in that it is not barely a speculative or rational thing, a cold, lifeless assent, a train of ideas in the head; it is also a disposition of heart. For thus saith the Scripture, "With the heart man believeth unto righteousness" and "If thou shalt confess with thy mouth the Lord Jesus, and shalt believe with thy heart that God hath raised Him from the dead, thou shalt be saved."

Christian faith is, then, not only an assent to the whole Gospel of Christ, but also a full reliance on the blood of Christ—a trust in the merits of His life, death, and resurrection, a recumbency upon Him as our atonement and our life as *given for us* and *living in us*. It is a sure confidence which a man has in God, that through the merits of Christ, his sins are forgiven and he is reconciled to the favor of God; and a cleaving to Him as our "wisdom, righteousness, sanctification, and redemption," or in one word, our salvation.

From Guilt and Power of Sin

What salvation is this? First, it is a *present* salvation. It is attainable on earth. Also, it is from sin—both from the guilt and the power of it. That is, from the guilt of all past sin. "There is, therefore, no condemnation now to them which" believe in Christ. And being saved from guilt, they are saved from fear—not from a filial fear of offending, but from all servile fear: fear of punishment, of the wrath of God. They are also saved from the fear, though not from the possibility, of falling away from the grace of God, and coming short of the great and precious promises. Thus, they have "peace with God through our Lord Jesus Christ" (Rom. 5:1) and are persuaded that "neither death, nor life, nor things present, nor things to come, nor height, nor depth, nor any other creature, shall be able to separate them from the love of God which is in Christ Jesus our Lord" (Rom. 8:38-39).

Through this faith they are also saved from the power of sin. So the apostle declares, "Whosoever abideth in Him sinneth not." Again, "Little children, let no man deceive you. He that committeth sin is of the devil." He that is, by faith, born of God, sins not by any habitual sin, for all habitual sin is sin reigning. But sin cannot reign in any that believes. Nor does he sin wilfully, for his will, while he abides in faith, is utterly set against all sin and abhors it as deadly poison. Nor is there sinful desire, for he continually desires the holy and perfect will of God, and any tendency to an unholy desire he stifles. Nor does he sin by infirmities, whether in act or thought, for his infirmities have no concurrence of his will, and without this they are not properly sins.

He who is thus justified, or saved, by faith is indeed born again of the Spirit unto a new life "which is hid with Christ in God." "He is a new creature: old things are passed away; all things in him are become new." And as a new-born babe he gladly receives the "sincere milk of the Word, and grows thereby"—going on in the might of the Lord his God from faith to faith, from grace to grace, until at length he comes into "a perfect man, unto the measure of the stature of the fulness of Christ."

Scriptural Christianity
"And they were all filled with the Holy Ghost"
(Acts 4:31).

The same expression occurs in the second chapter, "When the day of Pentecost was fully come, they were all [the apostles, with the women, and the mother of Jesus and His brethren] with one accord, in one place. And suddenly there came a sound from heaven, as of a rushing mighty wind. And there appeared unto them cloven tongues, like as of fire, and it sat upon each of them. And they were all filled with the Holy Ghost." One immediate effect was, "They began to speak with other tongues" so that the Parthians, Medes, Elamites, and other strangers who "came together, when this was noised abroad, heard them speak in their several tongues the wonderful works of God" (Acts 2:1-6).

In the present chapter we find no visible appearance,

as in the former instance, nor are we informed that the extraordinary gifts of the Holy Ghost were then given to any of them, such as the "gift of healing, of working other miracles, of prophecy, of discerning spirits, the speaking with divers kinds of tongues, and the interpretation of tongues" (1 Cor. 12:9-10).

Whether these gifts of the Holy Ghost were designed to remain in the church throughout all ages, and whether they will be restored at the nearer approach of the "restitution of all things" are questions which are not needful to decide. But it is needful to observe that even in the infancy of the church, God divided them with a sparing hand. Were all even then prophets? Were all workers of miracles? Had all the gift of healing? Did all speak with tongues? No, in no wise. Perhaps not one in a thousand. Probably none but the teachers in the church, and only some of them (1 Cor. 12:28-30). It was, therefore, for a more excellent purpose than this that "they were all filled with the Holy Ghost."

The Mind of Christ

It was to give them . . . the mind which was in Christ— those holy fruits of the Spirit—to fill them with "love, joy, peace, long-suffering, gentleness, goodness" (Gal. 5:22)—to endue them with faith, with meekness, and temperance—to enable them to crucify the flesh with its affections and lusts, its passions and desires and, in consequence of that inward change, to fulfill all outward righteousness, to walk as Christ also walked . . . in the work of faith, in the patience of hope, the labor of love (1 Thes. 1:3).

Where the Lord omnipotent takes to Himself His mighty power and reigns does He "subdue all things to Himself," cause every heart to overflow with love, and fill every mouth with praise. "Happy are the people that are in such a case; yea, blessed are the people who have the Lord for their God (Ps. 144:15). "Thou hast known that I, the Lord, am thy Saviour and thy Redeemer, the mighty God of Jacob. I have made thy officers peace and thy exacters righteousness. Violence shall no more be heard in the land, wasting nor destruction within thy borders; but thou shall call thy walls salvation and thy gates praise ... The sun shall be no more thy light by day: neither for brightness shall the moon give light unto thee: but the Lord shall be unto thee an everlasting light and thy God thy glory" (Isa. 60:16-19).

Where does this Christianity now exist? Where, I pray, do the Christians live? Which is the country where the inhabitants are all thus filled with the Holy Ghost? Let me ask you in tender love and in the spirit of meekness, "Is this a Christian city? Is scriptural Christianity found here? Are we considered as a community of men so 'filled with the Holy Ghost' as to enjoy in our hearts and show forth in our lives the genuine fruits of the Spirit? Are all the magistrates, all heads and governors of colleges and halls 'of one heart and soul'?"

For Those in Authority
In the fear and in the presence of the great God before whom both you and I shall shortly appear, I pray you that are in authority over us, whom I reverence for your offices' sake, to consider, are you "filled with the Holy Ghost"? Are all the thoughts of your hearts, all your tempers and desires suitable to your high calling? Ye venerable men who are especially called to form the tender minds of youth, to dispel the shades of ignor-

ance and error and train them up to be wise unto salvation, are you "filled with the Holy Ghost"? Do you continually remind those under your care that the one rational end of all our studies is to know, love, and serve the only true God and Jesus Christ whom He hath sent?

Many of us are more immediately called to minister in holy things. Are we patterns to the rest "in word, in conversation, in charity, in spirit, in faith, in purity"? (1 Tim. 4:12) Is there written on our forehead and on our heart "holiness to the Lord"? From what motives did we enter upon this office? Do we forsake and set aside, as much as in us lies, all worldly cares and studies? Are we apt to teach? Where are the "seals of our apostleship"?

For the Youth

What shall we say concerning the youth of this place? Have you either the form or the power of Christian godliness? Are you humble, teachable, advisable; or stubborn, self-willed, heady, and high-minded? Are you obedient to your superiors as to parents? Or do you despise those to whom you owe the tenderest reverence? Are you diligent in your business, pursuing your studies with all your strength? Do you redeem the time, crowding as much work into every day as it can contain? Or are you better managers of your future than of your time? Do you "remember the Sabbath Day to keep it holy"—to spend it in the more immediate worship of God? Do you know how to "possess your bodies in sanctification and honor"?

May it not be that many of you are a generation of triflers? How few of you spend from one week to another a single hour in private prayer? How few have any thought of God in the general tenor of your conversation!

Lord, save, or we perish! Take us out of the mire that we sink not! Oh help us against these enemies, for vain is the help of man. Unto Thee all things are possible. According to the greatness of Thy power, preserve Thou those that are appointed to die: and preserve us in the manner that seemeth to Thee good—not as we will, but as Thou wilt!

The Witness of the Spirit

"The Spirit itself beareth witness with our spirit, that we are the children of God" *(Romans 8:16)*.

How many vain, ignorant men have wrested this Scripture to the great loss, if not the destruction, of their souls? How many have mistaken the voice of their own imagination for this "witness of the Spirit of God," and thence idly presumed they were the children of God while they were doing the works of the devil? These are truly enthusiasts in the worse sense of the word.

Who can then be surprised if many reasonable men, seeing the dreadful effects of this delusion, and laboring to keep at the utmost distance from it, should sometimes lean towards another extreme?

Avoid Extremes

But is there any necessity for our running into one extreme or another? May we not steer a middle course and keep a sufficient distance from the spirit of error and enthusiasm without denying the gift of God and giving up the great privilege of His children?

What is this witness or testimony of our spirits? What is this testimony of God's Spirit? And how does He "bear witness with our spirit that we are the children of God"? And how is this joint testimony of God's Spirit and our own clearly distinguished from the presumption of a natural mind and from the delusion of the devil?

Let us first consider: What is the witness or testimony of our spirit? The foundation thereof is laid in numerous texts of Scripture. They are also collected and placed in the strongest light by many ancient and modern writers.

Among those foundations are the declarations of St. John in his First Epistle: "Hereby we know that we do know Him, if we keep His commandments" (2:3). "Whoso keepeth His word, in him verily is the love of God perfected: hereby know we that we are in Him" (2:5). "We know that we have passed from death to life, because we love the brethren" (3:14). These are some of the marks of the children of God. But how does it appear that we have these marks? How does it appear that we do love God and our neighbor and that we keep His commandments?

The answer might be the same as the answer to the question, How does it appear to you that you are alive? Are you not immediately conscious of it? By the same means you cannot but perceive if you love, rejoice, and delight in God. By the same you must be directly assured if you love your neighbor as yourself, if you are kindly affectioned to all mankind and full of gentleness and long-suffering. And with regard to the outward marks of the children of God, which is, according to St. John, the keeping of His commandments, you undoubtedly know in your breast if, by the grace of God, it belongs to you. Your conscience informs you from day to day if you do not take the name of God within your lips unless with seriousness and devotion or if you remember the Sabbath Day to keep it holy or honor your father and mother. This is properly the testimony of our own spirit—even of our own conscience.

An Inward Impression

But what is the testimony of God's Spirit who is superadded to and conjoined with this? How does He "bear witness with our spirit that we are the children of God?" It is hard to find words in the language of men to explain "the deep things of God." But one might say, the testimony of the Spirit is an inward impression on the soul whereby the Spirit of God witnesses to my spirit that I am a child of God—that Jesus Christ has loved me and given Himself for me and that all my sins are blotted out and I, even I, am reconciled to God.

That this testimony of the Spirit of God must needs, in the very nature of things, to be antecedent to the testimony of our own spirit may appear from this consideration: we must be holy of heart and holy in life before we can be conscious that we are so—before we can have the testimony of our own spirit that we are inwardly and outwardly holy. We must love God before we can be holy at all—this being the root of all holiness. We cannot love God till we know He loves us. "We love Him, because He first loved us." And we cannot know His pardoning love to us till His Spirit witnesses it to our spirit. Since this testimony of His Spirit must precede the love of God and all holiness, it must precede our inward consciousness or testimony of our spirit concerning them.

How, then, does the Spirit of God "bear witness with our spirit that we are the children of God" so as to exclude all doubt? The answer is clear from what has been observed above: as to the witness of our own spirit, the soul intimately perceives when it loves, delights, and rejoices in God—as when it loves and delights in anything on earth. He that now loves God delights and rejoices in Him with an humble joy and holy delight and obedient love. Thus, a Christian has an inward proof, which is nothing short of self-evidence.

The manner how the divine testimony is manifested to the heart I do not take upon me to explain. Such knowledge is too wonderful and excellent for me. The wind blows, and I hear the sound thereof, but I cannot tell how it comes or whither it goes. As no one knows the things of a man save the spirit of a man that is in him, so the manner of the things of God knows no one, save the Spirit of God. But the fact we know: the Spirit of God does give a believer such a testimony of his adoption that while it is present to the soul he can no more doubt the reality of his sonship than he can doubt the shining of the sun while he stands in the full blaze of its beams.

Neither Presumption nor Delusion

This joint testimony of God's Spirit and our spirit may also be clearly distinguished from the presumption of a natural mind and from the delusion of the devil. First, one who was never convinced of sin is always ready to flatter himself and think of himself, especially in spiritual things, more highly than he ought to think. Hence, it is in no wise strange if one who is vainly puffed up, when he hears of this privilege of true

Christians, would persuade himself he already possesses it.

But we may easily distinguish a child of God from a presumptuous self-deceiver. The Scriptures describe that joy in the Lord which accompanies His Spirit as an humble joy, a joy that abases to the dust—that makes a pardoned sinner cry out, "I am vile! What am I, or my father's house? Now my eye sees Thee, I abhor myself in dust and ashes!" And wherever lowliness is, there is meekness, patience, gentleness, long-suffering. There is a soft, yielding spirit, a mildness and sweetness, a tenderness of soul which words cannot express. But do these fruits attend the *supposed* testimony of the Spirit in a presumptuous man? Just the reverse. The more confident he is of the favor of God, the more he is lifted up, the more he exalts himself.

The Scriptures teach, "This is the love of God," the sure mark thereof, "that we keep His commandments" (1 John 5:3). Love rejoices to obey. A true lover of God hastens to do His will on earth as it is done in heaven. But the presumptuous pretender to the love of God takes the liberty to disobey the commandments of God. He is less zealous of good works, less watchful over his own heart, less jealous over his tongue. In a word, the whole form of his life is changed since he has fancied himself to be *at liberty*. He is no longer "exercising himself unto godliness." No, he has found an easier way to heaven—a broad, smooth flowery path. It follows with undeniable evidence that he has not the true testimony of his own spirit. He cannot be conscious of having those marks which he has not—that lowliness, meekness, and obedience. Nor yet can the Spirit of the God of Truth bear witness to a lie or testify that he is a child of God when he is manifestly a child of the devil.

How may one who has the real witness in himself distinguish it from presumption? How do you distinguish day from night or the light of a star or a glimmering taper from the light of the noonday sun? Do you not immediately and directly perceive that difference, provided your senses are rightly disposed? In like manner there is an inherent, essential difference between spiritual light and spiritual darkness and between the light wherewith the Sun of Righteousness shines upon our heart and that glimmering light which arises only from "sparks of our own kindling."

Suppose God were now to speak to any soul, "Thy sins are forgiven thee." He must be willing that that soul should know His voice; otherwise He would speak in vain. And that soul is absolutely assured, "This voice is the voice of God." Yet, he who has that witness in himself cannot explain it to one who has it not; nor is it to be expected that he should. Were there any natural medium to prove or natural method to explain the things of God to inexperienced men, then the natural man might discern the things of the Spirit of God. But this is utterly contrary to the assertion of the apostle that "he cannot know them because they are spiritually discerned."

Fruit as Evidence

How am I assured that I do not mistake the voice of the Spirit? Even by the testimony of my spirit—by "the answer of a good conscience towards God." By the fruits which He has wrought in your spirit, you shall know the testimony of the Spirit of God. Hereby you shall know you are in no delusion. The immediate fruits of the Spirit are "love, joy, peace, bowels of mercies, humbleness of mind, meekness, gentleness, long-suffering." And the outward fruits are the doing good to all men—the doing of no evil to any; and the walking in the light—a zealous, uniform obedience to all the commandments of God.

What of the inward witness? A verse preceding the text is very clear, "Ye have received, not the spirit of bondage, but the spirit of adoption, whereby we cry, Abba, Father," Is not this something *immediate* and *direct*—not the result of reflection or argumentation?

This is confirmed, not only by the experience of the children of God who can declare they never knew themselves to be in the favor of God, but by those who are convinced of sin, who feel the wrath of God abiding on them. These cannot be satisfied with anything less than a direct testimony from His Spirit that He is "merciful to their unrighteousness and remembers their sins and iniquities no more."

The sum of all is this: the testimony of the Spirit is an inward impression on the souls of believers whereby the Spirit of God directly testifies to their spirit that they are children of God. And it is not questioned whether there is a testimony of the Spirit, but whether there is any *direct* testimony. We believe there is, because this is the plain, natural meaning of the text as confirmed by the experience of innumerable children of God and by the experience of all who are convinced of sin, who can never rest till they have a direct witness, and even of the children of the world who, not having the witness in themselves, declare none can *know* his sins forgiven.

Two inferences may be drawn from the whole. The first, let none ever presume to rest in any supposed testimony of the Spirit which is separate from the fruit of it. And however this fruit may be clouded over for a while during the time of strong temptation, yet the substantial part of it remains, even under the thickest cloud.

The second inference is, let none rest in any supposed fruit of the Spirit without the witness. There may be foretastes of joy, of peace, of love, which are not delusive, but really from God long before the Spirit of God witnesses with our spirit that we have "redemption in the blood of Jesus, even . . . the forgiveness of sins." There may be a degree of long-suffering, of gentleness, of fidelity, meekness before we have a testimony of our acceptance. But it is by no means advisable to rest here; it is at the peril of our souls if we do. If we are wise, we shall be continually crying to God until His Spirit cries in our heart, *Abba Father!* This is the privilege of all the children of God, and without this we cannot retain a steady peace, nor avoid perplexing doubts and fears.

The Means of Grace
"Ye are gone away from Mine
ordinances and have not kept
them" *(Malachi 3:7).*

By *means of grace* I understand outward signs, words, or actions ordained of God and appointed for this end to be the ordinary channels whereby we might convey to men preventing, justifying, or sanctifying grace.

I use the expression *means of grace* because I know none better and because it has been generally used in the Christian church for many ages. The chief of these means are prayer, whether in secret or with the great congregation; searching the Scriptures (which implies reading, hearing, and meditating thereon); and receiving the Lord's Supper, eating bread and drinking wine in remembrance of Him. These we believe to be ordained of God as the ordinary channels of conveying His grace to the souls of men.

We allow that the whole value of the means depends on their actual subservience to the end of religion; consequently all these means, when separate from the end, are less than nothing and vanity. In fact, they are an abomination. Above all, if they are used as a kind of *commutation* for the religion they were designed to subserve, it is not easy to find words of the enormous folly and wickedness of thus turning God's arms against Himself.

Outward Means Not Enough

We allow likewise that all outward means whatever, if separate from the Spirit of God, cannot profit at all either to the knowledge or love of God. He alone by His own almighty power works in us what is pleasing in His sight. All outward things, unless He works in them and by them, are mere weak and beggarly elements. Whoever, therefore, imagines there is any intrinsic power in any means whatsoever does greatly err, not knowing the Scriptures, neither the power of God. We know that there is no inherent power in the words that are spoken in prayer, in the letters of Scripture read, the sound thereof heard, or the bread and wine received in the Lord's Supper. Rather it is God along who is the Giver of every good gift, the Author of all grace. We know likewise that He is able to give the same grace though there were no means on the face of the earth. In this sense we may affirm that with God there is no such thing as means, as He is equally able to work whatsoever pleases Him by any, or by none at all.

We allow further that the use of all means will never atone for sin—that it is the blood of Christ alone whereby any sinner can be reconciled to God, there being no other propitiation for our sins, no other fountain for sin and for uncleanness. Every believer in Christ is deeply convinced that there is no merit in him nor in any of his own works or in uttering prayer or searching the Scripture or hearing the Word of God or eating of the bread and drinking of the cup. Christ is the only means of grace.

Yet, we allow that a large proportion of those who are called Christians abuse the means of grace to the destruction of their own souls. This is doubtless the case with all those who rest content in the form of godliness, without the power. Either they fondly presume they are Christians already because they do thus and so, or else they suppose they shall infallibly be so because they use these means, idly dreaming there is some power therein whereby they shall certainly be made holy, or that there is a sort of merit in using them which will surely move God to give them holiness or accept them without it.

Little do these understand that great foundation of the whole Christian building, "By grace are ye saved." But the main question remains, How may I attain thereto? If you say, "Believe and thou shalt be saved," one answers, "But how shall I be saved?" You reply, "Wait upon God." But how is one to wait? In the means of grace or out of them? Does one wait for the grace of God which brings salvation by using means, or by laying them aside?

God's Guidance Described

It cannot possibly be conceived that the Word of God should give no direction on such an important point. In fact, we have only to consult the oracles of God. According to these, all who desire the grace of God are to wait for it in the means which He has ordained—in using, not in laying them aside.

First, all who desire the grace of God are to wait for it in prayer. This is the express direction of our Lord Himself. In His Sermon upon the Mount, after explaining at large wherein religion consists, He adds, "Ask and it shall be given you; seek and you shall find; knock and it shall be opened to you" (Matt. 7:7).

That no doubt might remain, our Lord labors this point in a more peculiar manner. He appeals to every man's own heart. "What man is there of you, whom if his son ask bread, will he give him a stone? Or if he ask a fish, will he give a serpent? If ye then, being evil, know how to give good gifts unto your children, how much more shall your Father which is in heaven give good things to them that ask Him?" (vv. 9-11)

The absolute necessity of using the means of prayer if we would receive any gift from God further appears in the words of our Lord by parable and by direct injunction.

Secondly, all who desire the grace of God are to wait for it in searching the Scriptures. Our Lord's direction here is likewise plain and clear. "Search the Scriptures," says He to the unbelieving Jews, "for they testify of Me" (John 5:39). That a blessing of God attends the use of this means appears from what is recorded concerning the Bereans, who, after hearing St. Paul, "searched the Scriptures daily." Therefore, many of them believed and found grace in God in the way which He had ordained (Acts 17:11-12).

This is also a means whereby God confirms and increases true wisdom, as we learn from Paul's words to Timothy, "From a child thou hast known the Holy Scriptures which are able to make thee wise unto salvation through faith which is in Christ Jesus" (2 Tim. 3:15). The same truth—that this is the great means God has ordained for conveying His manifold grace to man—is delivered in the fullest manner that can be conceived with words which immediately follow, "All Scripture is given by inspiration of God, and is profitable . . . to the end that the man of God may be perfect, thoroughly furnished unto all good works" (vv. 16-17).

Thirdly, all who desire an increase of the grace of God are to wait for it by partaking of the Lord's Supper, for it is also a direction God Himself has given. "The same night in which He was betrayed, He took bread, and brake it, and said, 'Take, eat; this is My body [That is, the sacred sign of My body]. This do in remembrance of Me . . .' Likewise, He took the cup, saying, 'This cup is the new testament [the sacred sign of that covenant]; this do in remembrance of Me. For as often as ye eat this bread and drink this cup you do show forth the Lord's death till He come'" (1 Cor. 11:23ff). Thus, you testify by these visible signs before God, angels, and men. You manifest your solemn remembrance of His death till He comes in the clouds of heaven. Only let a man first examine himself whether he understands the nature and design of this holy institution and whether he really desires to be made conformable to the death of Christ.

Objections Answered

But as plainly as God has pointed out the way, so innumerable objections have been raised against it. One is that you cannot use these means without *trusting* in them. If this were true, Christ must have known it and would have warned us. But there is no hint of this in the whole revelation of Jesus Christ. Also, it is objected that this is seeking salvation by works. But how is either of these implied by waiting in the way God has ordained?

It has also been urged vehemently that Christ is the *only* means of grace. I answer this is a man playing upon words. Explain your term and the objection vanishes away. When we say "prayer is a means of grace," we understand *a channel through which the grace of God is conveyed.* When you say "Christ is the means of grace," you understand *the sole price and purchase of it.*

Some have asked, "But does not the Scripture direct us to *wait* for salvation? Does not David say, 'My soul waiteth upon God, for of Him cometh my salvation'?" This cannot be denied; since it is the gift of God, we are undoubtedly to *wait* on Him for salvation. But how shall we wait? If God Himself has appointed a way, can you find a better way of waiting for Him? In this very way did David wait as his own words testify, "I have waited for Thy saving health, Oh Lord, and have kept Thy law. Teach me, oh Lord, the way of Thy statutes, and I shall keep it unto the end."

They who desire the grace of God are, therefore, to wait for it in the means He has ordained. As we find no command in the Bible for any particular order to be observed, so neither do the providence and Spirit of God adhere to any without variation. The means into which different men are led and in which they find the blessing of God are varied. Still, our wisdom is to follow the leadings of His providence and His Spirit. And in the meantime, the sure and general rule for all who groan for the salvation of God is this—Whenever opportunity serves, use all the means which God has ordained, for who knows in which means God will choose to meet you with the grace that alone brings salvation?

As to the manner of using them, it behooves us first always to retain a lively sense that God is above all means. Have a care, therefore, of limiting the Almighty. He does whatever and whenever pleases Him. He can convey His grace either in or out of any of the means which He has appointed. Before you use any means, let it be deeply impressed upon your soul there is no *power* in this. But because God bids, therefore I do. Because He directs me to wait in this way, here I wait for His free mercy whereof comes my salvation.

In using all means, seek God alone. In and through every outward thing, look singly to the *power* of His Spirit and the merits of His own. Nothing short of God can satisfy your soul. If God was there, if His love flowed into your heart, you have forgotten as it were, the outward work. You see, you know, you feel that God is all in all. Sink down before Him! Give Him all the praise.

On Christian Perfection
"Not as though I had already attained,
either were already perfect"
(Philippians 3:12).

"Let us go on unto perfection"
(Hebrews 6:1).

There is scarcely any expression in the Bible that has given more offense than this. The word *perfect* is what many cannot bear. The very sound of it is an abomination to them. And whoever *preaches perfection*, namely, asserts that it is attainable in this life, runs great hazard of being accounted by them worse than a heathen or a publican.

Whatsoever God has spoken, that will we speak, whether men will hear or whether they will forbear, knowing that then alone can any minister of Christ be "pure from the blood of all men."

We may not, therefore, lay these expressions aside, seeing they are the words of God and not of man. But we ought to explain the meaning of them, that those who are sincere may not err to the right hand or left. This is the more needful to be done, because in the verse already repeated the apostle speaks of himself as not perfect. And yet immediately after, in Philippians 3:15, he speaks of himself and many others as perfect: "Let us, as many as be perfect, be thus minded." I shall endeavor to show in what sense Christians are *not*, and in what sense they *are* perfect.

Imperfect in Knowledge and Judgment

In the first place, from both experience and Scripture it appears that they are not perfect in knowledge; they are not so perfect in this life as to be free from ignorance. Touching the Almighty, they cannot search Him out to perfection. Neither is it for them to know the times and seasons when God will work His great works upon the earth. They know not the reasons even of many of His present dispensations with the sons of men. Yea, often with regard to His dealings with them, God says, "What I do, thou knowest not now; but thou shalt know hereafter." So great is the ignorance, so very little the knowledge of even the best of men!

No one, then, is so perfect in this life as to be free from ignorance. Nor, secondly, from mistake, which indeed is almost an unavoidable consequence of it. It is true the children of God do not mistake as to the things essential to salvation, for they are "taught of God"; and the way which He teaches them, the way of holiness, is so plain that "The wayfaring man, though a fool, need not err therein." But in things unessential to salvation they do err, and that frequently.

With regard to the Holy Scriptures themselves, as careful as they are to avoid it, the best of men are liable to mistake. Even the children of God are not agreed as to the interpretation of many places in Holy Writ, nor is their difference of opinion any proof that they are not the children of God on either side. But it is proof that we are no more to expect any living man to be infallible than to be omniscient. When St. John, speaking to his brethren, said, "Ye have an unction from the Holy One, and ye know all things," (1 John 2:20) the answer is plain: "Ye know all things that are needful for your soul's health." That the apostle never designed to extend this farther—that he could not speak in an absolute sense is clear, otherwise he would describe the disciple as "above his Master," seeing that Christ Himself, as man, knew not all things: "Of that hour," said he, "knoweth no man, no, not the Son, but the Father only." His oft-repeated caution, "Let no man deceive you," was to those very persons who had the unction from the Holy One.

As Christians are not so perfect as to be free from ignorance or error, neither are they free from infirmities. Only let us take care to understand this word aright. I mean here not only those which are properly termed *bodily infirmities,* but all those inward and outward imperfections which are not of a moral nature. Such are weakness or slowness of understanding, dullness or confusedness of apprehension, incoherency of thought, irregular quickness or heaviness of imagination. Such is the want of a ready or retentive memory. Other kinds are slowness of speech, impropriety of language, ungracefulness of pronunciation, to which one might add a thousand defects, either in conversation or behavior. These are the infirmities which are found in the best of men in a larger or smaller proportion. From these we cannot hope to be perfectly free till the Spirit returns to God that gave it.

Not Freedom from Temptation

Nor can we expect till then to be wholly free from temptation. Such perfection belongs not to this life. It is true there are those who, being given up to work all uncleanness with greediness, scarce perceive the temptations which they resist not, and so seem to be without temptation.

There are also many whom the wise enemy of souls, seeing to be fast asleep in the dead form of godliness, will not tempt to gross sin, lest they should awake before they drop into everlasting burnings. I know there are also children of God who, being now justified freely, having found redemption in the blood of Christ, for the present feel no temptation. But this state will not last always, as we may learn from the single consideration that the Son of God Himself, in the days of His flesh, was tempted, even to the end of His life.

In what sense, then, are Christians perfect? It should be premised that there are several stages in the Christian life, as in natural: some are newborn babes, others have attained to more maturity.

Not Servants of Sin

Now the Word of God plainly declares that even those who are justified, who are born again, do not "continue in sin," that they cannot "live any longer therein" (Rom. 6:1-2), that they are "planted together in the likeness of His death" (v.5); that their "old man is crucified with Him," the body of sin being destroyed, so that henceforth they do not serve sin, that being dead with Christ they are free from sin (vv. 6-7), that they are "dead unto sin and alive unto God," (v. 11), that "sin hath nor more dominion over them," who are "not under the law, but under grace," that these "being free from sin are become the servants of righteousness" (vv. 14, 18).

The very least which can be implied in these words is that persons spoken of therein, all real Christians, or believers in Christ, are made free from outward sin. And the same freedom which St. Paul here expresses in such variety of phrases, St. Peter expresses in 1 Peter 4:1-2: "He that hath suffered in the flesh hath ceased from sin—that he no longer should live to the desires of men, but to the will of God." This ceasing from sin, if it be interpreted in the lowest sense, must denote ceasing from the outward act, from any transgression of the Law.

Most expressive are the well-known words of St. John in the third chapter of his First Epistle. "He that committeth sin is of the devil, for the devil sinneth from the beginning. For this purpose the Son of God was manifested, that He might destroy the works of the devil. Whosoever is born of God doth not commit sin, for His seed remaineth in him and he cannot sin because he is born of God."

Objections Answered by Scripture

It is said this means only that he sins not *wilfully,* or he does not commit sin *habitually* or *not as other men do* or *not as he did before.* But by whom is this said? By St. John? No, there is no such word in the text, nor in the whole chapter nor in all this epistle nor in any part of his writings whatsoever. The best way, then, to answer a bold assertion is simply to deny it. And if any man can prove it from the Word of God, let him bring forth his strong reasons.

Some have said, "Did not Abraham himself commit sin, prevaricating and denying his wife? Did not Moses commit sin when he provoked God at the waters of strife? Did not even David, 'the man after God's own heart' commit sin in the matter of Uriah the Hittite— even murder and adultery?" It is most sure he did. But what is it you would infer from hence? It may be granted that the holiest men among the Jews did sometimes commit sin. But if you would infer that all Christians do and must commit sin as long as they live, this consequence we utterly deny. It will never follow from those premises.

Those who argue thus seem never to have considered the declaration of our Lord, "Verily, I say unto you, among them that are born of women there hath not risen a greater than John the Baptist; notwithstanding, he that is least in the kingdom of heaven is greater than he" (Matt 11:11). The "kingdom of heaven" here is that kingdom of God on earth whereunto all true believers in Christ belong. In these words our Lord declares that before His coming in the flesh, there had not been one greater than John the Baptist (which includes Abraham and David). Therefore we cannot measure the privilege of real Christians by those formerly given to the Jews.

The apostles themselves, it is said, committed sin—even the greatest of them, Peter and Paul: St. Paul by his sharp contentions with Barnabas and St. Peter by his dissimulation at Antioch. Suppose Peter and Paul did then commit sin; what would you infer from that? That all other apostles committed sins sometimes? There is no shadow of proof in this. Or would you infer that all other Christians of the apostolic age committed sin? That is worse. Nowhere do you see that any man *must* commit sin at all.

We said that St. Paul besought the Lord thrice and yet he could not escape from temptation, as he said, "There was given to me a thorn in the flesh . . . touching this I besought the Lord thrice that it might depart from me. And He said unto me, 'My grace is sufficient for thee.'" Let it be observed, it does not appear that this thorn, whatever it was, occasioned St. Paul to commit sin. The ancient fathers inform us it was bodily pain or grievous torments of the body. The apostle's own words seem to agree with this. But whatever it was, it could not be inward or outward sin.

I call you all to record this day, who find the strength of Christ resting upon you. Can you glory in anger or pride or lust? Can you take pleasure in these infirmities? Do these weaknesses make you strong? Would you not leap into hell, were it possible, to escape them?

By yourselves, then, judge whether the apostle could glory and take pleasure in them.

How shall we reconcile St. John with himself? In one place he declares, "Whosoever is born of God doth not commit sin," and again, "If we say that we have no sin, we deceive ourselves and the truth is not in us," and again, "If we say that we have not sinned, we make Him a liar."

But the difficulty here vanishes when we see "If we say we have no sin" is explained by the latter verse, "If we say we have not sinned." Also, the point under present consideration is not whether we *have* or *have not sinned heretofore.* And a later verse explains both, "If we confess our sins, He is faithful and just to forgive us our sins and to cleanse us from all unrighteousness." It is as if he had said, "I have before affirmed 'the blood of Jesus Christ cleanses us from all sin,' but let no man say, I need it not."

The apostle resumes this subject in another chapter and largely explains his own meaning. "Little children, let no man deceive you. He that doeth righteousness is righteous, even as He is righteous. He that committeth sin is of the devil, for the devil sinneth from the beginning. For this purpose the Son of God was manifested, that He might destroy the works of the devil. Whosoever is born of God doth not commit sin, for His seed remaineth in him and he cannot sin because he is born of God" (1 John 3:7-9). In conformity both to the doctrine of St. John and the whole tenor of the New Testament, *a Christian is so far perfect as not to commit sin.*

This is the glorious privilege of every Christian—yea though he be but a *babe in Christ.* But it is only of those who *are strong* in the Lord "and have overcome the wicked one." They are in such a sense perfect as to be freed from evil thoughts and evil tempers. Here let it be observed that thoughts concerning evil are not always evil thoughts. A man, for instance, may think of a murder which another has committed and yet this is no evil or sinful thought.

If the heart is no longer evil, evil thoughts can no longer proceed out of it. Christians are also freed from evil tempers. This is evident from the declaration of our Lord Himself, "The disciple is not above his Master; but everyone that is perfect shall be as his Master."If the Lord suffered, we should be content to follow in His steps. As the Master was free of evil tempers, so is His disciple, even every real Christian.

Everyone of these can say with St. Paul, "I am crucified with Christ; nevertheless I live; yet not I, but Christ liveth in me"—words that manifestly describe a deliverance from inward as well as from outward sin.

Heart Purity the Goal
He, therefore, who lives as a true believer, has purified his heart by faith, insomuch that every one that has Christ in him, the hope of glory, "purifieth himself, even as He is pure" (1 John 3:3). He is purified from pride, for Christ was lowly of heart. He is pure from self-will, or desire, for Christ desired only to do the will of His Father. And he is pure from anger, in the common sense of the word, for Christ was meek and gentle, patient and long-suffering. (I say in the common sense of the word, for all anger is not evil.)

Thus, Jesus saves His people from their sins—not only from outward sins but also from the sins of their hearts. "True," say some, "we shall be saved from our sins, but not till death—not in this world." But how are we to reconcile this with the express words of St. John? "Herein is our love made perfect, that we may have boldness in the day of judgment: because as He is, so are we in the world."

Thus has the Lord fulfilled the things. He spoke by His holy prophets—by Moses in particular saying, I "will circumcise thine heart and the heart of thy seed to love the Lord thy God with all thy heart and with all thy soul (Deut. 30:6); and by David crying out, "Create in me a clean heart, and renew a right spirit within me"; and most remarkably by Ezekiel, "Then will I sprinkle clean water upon you, and you shall be clean—from all your filthiness and from all your idols will I cleanse you. A new heart also will I give you and a new spirit will I put within you" (Ezek. 36:25-26).

"Having, therefore, these promises, dearly beloved," both in the Law and in the prophets, and having the prophetic word confirmed unto us in the Gospel by our blessed Lord and His apostles, "let us cleanse ourselves from all filthiness of flesh and spirit, perfecting holiness in the fear of God."

Let us press towards the mark for the prize of the high calling of God in Christ Jesus, "crying unto Him day and night till we also are delivered from the bondage of corruption into the glorious liberty of the sons of God!"

The Use of Money

"I say unto you, Make to yourselves friends of the mammon of unrighteousness, that when ye fail, they may receive you into everlasting habitations" *(Luke 16:9).*

An excellent branch of Christian wisdom is here inculcated by our Lord on all His followers, namely, the use of money. It has been the manner of poets, orators, and philosophers in almost all ages and nations to rail at money as the grand corrupter of the world, the bane of virtue, the pest of human society.

The fault does not lie in the money, but in them that use it. It may be used ill or well—and what may not? It is of unspeakable service to all civilized nations in all the common affairs of life; it is a most compendious instrument of transacting all manner of business and of doing all manner of good. In the present state of mankind it is an excellent gift of God answering the noblest ends.

In the hands of His children it is food for the hungry, drink for the thirsty, raiment for the naked. It gives the traveler or the stranger a place to lay his head. It may be a means of health to the sick, of ease to that are in pain. It may be as eyes to the blind and as feet to the lame. It is therefore of the highest concern that all who fear God know how to employ this valuable talent.

Three plain rules are sufficient for faithful stewards of "the mammon of unrighteousness."

Gain All You Can
First, "gain all you can." Here we may speak like children of the world. We ought to gain all we can without paying more for gold than it is worth. We ought not to gain money at the expense of life nor at the expense of our health. Therefore we ought not to enter in any employment which is so difficult as to impair our constitution. Neither should we engage in business which deprives us of proper seasons for food and sleep.

In gaining all we can, we ought not to hurt our mind

by defrauding the king, cheating, or lying; neither should we hurt our neighbor by taking advantage of him or enticing his servants or workmen. We should not sell our neighbor anything that would impair his health. Certainly, we will not hurt our neighbor in his soul by ministering to his unchastity or to his intemperance.

These cautions and restrictions being observed, "gain all you can." Gain all you can by honest industry. Use all possible diligence. Lose no time. If you understand yourself and your relation to God and man, you know you have none to spare. Never leave anything till tomorrow which you can do today. And do it as well as possible. Do not sleep or yawn over it; put your whole strength to the work. Spare no pains. Let nothing be done in a slight and careless manner. Gain all you can by using in your business all the understanding which God has given you. You should be continually learning from the experience of others or from your own experience, reading, or reflection, to do everything you have to do better today than you did yesterday.

Save All You Can
Having gained all you can by honest wisdom and unwearied diligence, the second rule of Christian prudence is, "save all you can."

Do not waste any part of so precious a talent merely in gratifying the desires of the flesh. I do not mean avoid gluttony and drunkenness only, but there is a regular, reputable kind of sensuality, an elegant epicurism which does not immediately disorder the stomach nor impair the understanding, and yet it cannot be maintained without considerable expense.

Despise delicacy; be content with what plain nature requires.

Do not waste merely in gratifying the desire of the eye by superfluous or expensive apparel or by needless ornaments. Waste no part of it in curiously adorning your houses, in superfluous, expensive furniture, in costly paintings, in elegant rather than useful gardens. Lay out nothing to gratify the pride of life, to gain the admiration or praise of men.

And why should you throw away money upon your children any more than upon yourself in delicate food or costly apparel in superfluities of any kind? Why should you purchase for them more pride or lust, more vanity or foolish and hurtful desires? Why increase their temptations and snares? Do not leave it to them to throw away. How amazing is the infatuation of parents who think they can never leave their children enough. "What should you do if you have a considerable fortune to leave?" I know what I *ought* to do. If I had one child who knew the value of money, who I believed would put it to true use, I should think it my duty to leave that child the bulk of my fortune and the rest just so much as would enable them to live in that manner they had been accustomed to. "But what if your children were equally ignorant of the true use of money?" I ought then to give each what would keep him above want and to bestow the rest in such a manner as I judged would be most for the flory of God.

Give All You Can

But we are not to stop here. Not only are you to gain and save all you can, you are to "give all you can." As you are not your own, but His, such is, likewise, all you enjoy. The directions which God has given us touching the use of our worldly substance may be comprised in the following particulars. If you desire to be a faithful and wise steward out of that portion of your Lord's goods which he has lodged in your hands, first provide things needful for yourself—food and raiment and whatever nature moderately requires for perserving the body in health and strength. Also, provide these for your wife, your children, your servants, or any others of your household. If, when this is done, there is a surplus, then "do good to them that are of the household of faith." If there is still a surplus, "as you have opportunity, do good unto all men."

If a doubt should arise in your mind concerning what you should spend on yourself or your family, calmly inquire: (1) In expending this sum, am I acting according to my character? Am I acting as a steward of my Lord's goods? (2) Am I doing this in obedience to His Word? (3) Can I offer up this action as a sacrifice to God through Jesus Christ? (4) Have I reason to believe that for this I shall have a reward at the resurrection of the just? By this fourfold consideration you will receive clear light as to the way you should go.

If any doubt still remains, you may further examine yourself by prayer. See whether you can say to the Searcher of hearts, "Lord, Thou knowest I act with a single eye as a steward of Thy goods. Let this be a holy sacrifice acceptable through Jesus Christ." Now if your conscience bears you witness in the Holy Ghost that this prayer is well pleasing to God, then you have no reason to doubt.

You see, then, what it is to "make yourselves friends of the mammon of unrighteousness." Brethren, can we be either wise or faithful stewards unless we thus manage our Lord's goods?

On Eternity

"From everlasting to everlasting,
Thou art God" *(Psalm 90:2).*

How can we grasp this awful subject? It is so vast that the narrow mind of man is utterly unable to comprehend it. But does it not bear some affinity to another incomprehensible thing, immensity? May not space be compared with duration? But what is immensity? It is boundless space. And what is eternity? It is boundless duration.

Eternity has generally been considered as divisible into two parts: that eternity which is past and that which is to come. Some may think it is not strictly proper to say there is an eternity that is past. But the meaning is easily understood: we mean duration which had no beginning, as by eternity to come we mean that duration which will have no end. It is God alone who "inhabiteth eternity" in both these senses. The great Creator alone is "from everlasting to everlasting."

Time as Duration

What is time? Is it not a fragment of eternity broken off at both ends—that portion of duration which commenced when the world began, which will continue as long as the world endures, and then expire forever? It is that portion which is at present measured by the revolution of the sun and planets.

But by what means can a mortal man, the creature of a day, form an idea of eternity? What bears any resemblance to it?

Let us turn our thoughts to duration without end. He has imparted this not only to angels and archangels and all the companies of heaven, but also to the inhabitants of the earth who dwell in houses of clay. Their bodies indeed are "crushed before the moth," but their souls will never die.

Perhaps we may go a step further: is not matter itself, as well as spirit, in one sense eternal? Not, as some philosophers have dreamed, that anything existed from eternity, except God. All matter is continually changing, but that it is changeable does not imply it is perishable. The substance may remain one and the same, though under innumerable forms. The heavens themselves will be dissolved; "the elements shall melt with fervent heat." But they will be only dissolved, not destroyed. They will melt, but they will not perish.

To form a more adequate conception of eternity, let us compare it with several degrees of duration which we are acquainted with. Suppose there were a ball of sand as large as the globe of earth. Suppose a grain of this sand were to be annihilated in a thousand years. Yet the duration wherein this ball would be annihilated at the rate of one grain in a thousand years would bear infinitely less proportion to eternity than a single grain of sand would bear to the mass.

Consider another comparison. Suppose the ocean to be enlarged to include all the space between the earth and the starry heavens. Suppose a drop of this water to be annihilated once in a thousand years. Yet the duration wherein this ocean would be annihilated in this process would be infinitely less, in proportion to eternity, than one drop of water to that whole ocean.

Look again at the immortal spirits in this or the other world. When they shall have lived thousands of thousands—yea millions of ages—their duration will be but just begun. They will be only upon the threshold of eternity.

Endless Happiness or Misery

There is another dimension of eternity which is of unspeakable importance as it relates to immortal spirits. That is either a happy or miserable eternity. The inhabitants of heaven continually cry, "Holy, holy, holy is the Lord, the God, the Almighty, who was, and who is, and who is to come!" When millions of ages have elapsed, their eternity is but just begun. On the other hand, in what condition are those immortal spirits who have made choice of a miserable eternity. Suppose one to plunge just now into "the lake of fire burning with brimstone, where they have no rest, day or night." To be chained there one day or one hour would seem like a long time. But after thousands of thousands of years he has but begun to taste of his bitter cup.

How foolish—even mad—it is for one with under-standing to prefer deliberately temporal things to eternal. How contrary to all reason to prefer the happiness of a year to the happiness of eternity, especially when the refusing of a happy eternity implies the choosing of a miserable eternity, for there cannot be any medium between everlasting joy and everlasting pain.

Some have entertained the vain thought that death will put an end to the soul as well as the body. But it will put an end to neither; it will only alter the manner of their existence. When the body "returns to become dust as it was before, the spirit will return to God that gave it."

Faith in the Unseen Needful

Yet the unspeakable folly, this unutterable madness of preferring present things to eternal is the disease of every man born into the world while in his natural state. The mind does not see either the beauties or the terrors of eternity, because they are so distant from us. It is as if they had no existence. Meanwhile, we are wholly taken up with things present till our nature is changed by grace.

A remedy is provided for this blindness to futurity. It is faith—defined by the apostle as "an evidence," or conviction—"of things not seen." This alone opens the eyes of the understanding to see God and the things of God. Faith places the unseen, the eternal world continually before his face.

What then can be a fitter employment for a wise man than to meditate upon these things—frequently to expand his thoughts "beyond the bounds of this diurnal sphere," and to expatiate above even the starry heavens in the field of eternity? What a means might it be to confirm his contempt of the poor, little things of earth?

When a man of huge possessions was boasting to his friend of the largeness of his estate, Socrates desired him to bring a map of the earth and to point out Attica therein. When this was done, he next asked Alcibiades to point out his own estate therein. When he could not do this because it was so small, it was easy to observe how trifling the possessions were. How applicable is this to the present case.

Eternal bliss or pain! Everlasting happiness or everlasting misery! One would think it would swallow up every other thought in every reasonable creature. Certainly it ought to do so. If these things are true, there can be but one thing needful. Let us, whatever others do, choose that better part which shall never be taken from us!

On the Fall of Man
"Dust thou art, and unto dust shalt thou return"
(Genesis 3:19).

Why is there *pain* in the world, since God is "loving to every man and His mercy is over all His works"? Because there is *sin.* Had there been no sin there would have been no pain. But pain is the necessary effect of sin. But why is there sin in the world? Because man was created in the image of God; he is not mere matter, a clod of earth, a lump of clay without sense or understanding, but a spirit like his Creator, not only with sense and understanding, but also a will exerting itself in various affections.

Man a Free Moral Agent
To crown all the rest, he was endued with liberty, a power of directing his own affections and actions, a capacity of choosing good and evil. Had not man been endued with this, all the rest would have been of no use. Had he not been a free, as well as an intelligent being, his understanding would have been incapable of holiness or any kind of virtue. And having this power of choosing good or evil, he chose the latter. Thus sin entered the world and pain of every kind preparatory to death.

But this plain, single account of the origin of evil was not discoverable by all the wisdom of man till it pleased God to reveal it to the world. Till then man was a mere enigma to himself—a riddle which none but God could solve.

First, note the intelligence and subtlety of the serpent. Eve was not startled and frightened at hearing the serpent *speak* and *reason*; hence she must have known that reason and speech were the original properties of the serpent. She entered into conversation with him as he began to lie about God, "Ye shall not surely die, for God doth know that in the day ye eat thereof your eyes shall be opened and ye shall be as gods, knowing good and evil." Here sin began in unbelief. "The woman was deceived," said the apostle. She believed a lie. And unbelief brought forth actual sin.

But the man, as the apostle observes, was not deceived. He sinned with his eyes open. If this was the case, it is not absurd to believe that Adam sinned in his heart before he sinned outwardly by eating of the forbidden fruit. He loved the creature before the Creator.

Unhappiness Followed Sin

Immediately pain followed sin. When man lost his innocence, he lost his happiness. He painfully feared God in whom his supreme happiness previously consisted. Even then God dealt tenderly with the pair, although they began to blame each other and the serpent. In the midst of judgment, God remembered mercy by promising a Redeemer who would bruise the serpent's head. Unto the woman He said, "I will greatly multiply thy sorrow . . . in pain thou shalt bring forth children." And unto Adam He said, "In the sweat of thy face shalt thou eat bread till thou return to the ground . . . dust thou art and unto dust thou shalt return."

Man is dust, but how fearfully and wonderfully wrought into innumerable fibers, nerves, membranes, muscles, arteries. But since he sinned he is mortal, corruptible dust. By sad experience we find that this "corruptible body presses down the soul" and frequently hinders its operations. Yet the soul cannot dispense with its service, imperfect as it is.

"Unto dust thou shalt return." How admirably well has the wise Creator secured the execution of this sentence on all the offspring of Adam! It is true that Enoch and Elijah escaped death, but great masters of the art of healing have been unable to prevent the gradual decays of nature. All their boasted skills cannot heal old age or hinder dust from returning to dust. The days of man for about three thousand years have been fixed at three-score years and ten.

God has indeed provided for the execution of His own decree in the very principles of our nature. Look around and see the darkness, ignorance, error, and vice in ten thousand forms; see consciousness of guilt, fear, sorrow, shame, and remorse covering the face of the earth. See misery, the daughter of sin. See on every side sickness and pain and the inhabitants of every nation driving the helpless sons of men to the gates of death.

God's Invasion of the World

But can the Creator despise the work of His own hands? "God so loved the world that He gave His . . . Son." Here is a remedy provided for all our guilt. "He bore our sins in His body on the tree." And "if anyone has sinned, he has an Advocate with the Father, Jesus Christ the righteous."

God has also, through the intercession of His Son, given us His Holy Spirit to renew us both in knowledge and also in His moral image." This being done, we know that "all things work together for our good." All natural evils change their nature; sorrow, sickness, and pain will all prove medicines to heal our spiritual sickness.

Behold, then, both the justice and mercy of God—His justice in punishing sin, the sin in him in whose loins we were all then contained, on Adam and his posterity, and His mercy in providing a universal remedy for a universal evil—in appointing the second Adam to die for all who had died in the first.

It should be observed that "where sin abounded, grace does much more abound." We may gain infinitely more than we have lost. We may now attain higher degrees of holiness and glory than it would have been possible for us to attain without a Redeemer.

On Divine Providence

"Even the very hairs of your head are all numbered" (*Luke 12:7*).

The doctrine of Divine providence has been received by wise men in all ages and is acknowledged today in most parts of the world—even among barbarous nations. Yet the conception of a divine providence has been dark, confused, and imperfect.

And it is no wonder, for only God Himself can give a clear, consistent, perfect account of His manner of governing the world. In the verses preceding the text, our Lord has been arming His disciples against the fear of man: "Be not afraid of them that kill the body and after that have no more that they can do." He guards them against this fear, first by reminding them of what was infinitely more terrible than anything which man could inflict: "Fear him, who after he hath killed, hath power to cast into hell." He guards them further against it by considering an overruling providence, by speaking of the sparrows, "Not one of them shall fall to the ground without your Father. But the very hairs of your head are numbered."

Governor and Sustainer

This need not imply that God does literally number the hairs on the heads of all His creatures, but it does imply that nothing is so small or insignificant in the sight of men as not to be an object of care and providence of God. There is scarcely any doctrine in the whole compass of revelation which is of deeper importance than this.

The eternal, almighty, all-wise, all-gracious God is the Creator of heaven and earth. He called out of nothing by His all-powerful Word the whole universe. And after he had set all things else in array—the plants after their kinds, fish and fowl, beasts and reptiles after their kinds, "He created man after His own image." And He saw that all things together were "very good."

As this all-wise, all-gracious Being created all things, so He sustains all things. He is the Preserver as well as the Creator of everything that exists. "He upholdeth all things by the Word of His power"—that is, by His powerful Word. It must be that He knows everything He has made and everything He preserves from moment to moment; otherwise He could not preserve it.

If the eye of man discerns things at a small distance, the eye of an eagle at a greater, and the eye of an angel at ten thousand times greater distance, shall not the eye of God see everything through the whole extent of creation?

True, our narrow understanding but imperfectly comprehends this. But as He created and sustains all things, He is present at all times, in all places. He "besets us behind and before." We acknowledge "such knowledge is too high" and wonderful for us; we "cannot attain unto it." The manner of His presence no man can explain, nor probably can any angel in heaven.

The omnipresent God sees and knows all the properties of the beings He has made. He knows all the connections, dependencies, and relations, and all the ways in which one of them can affect another. In particular, He saw all the inanimate parts of the creation . . . He knows how the stars, comets, or planets above influence the inhabitants of the earth beneath.

He knows all the animals of the lower world, whether beasts, birds, fish, reptiles, or insects; He knows all the qualities and powers He has given them. He knows every good angel and every evil angel and looks from heaven upon the children of men over the whole face of the earth. He knows all the hearts of the sons of men and understands all their thoughts. He sees what any angel, devil, man, either thinks or speaks or does—yea, and all they feel. He sees all their sufferings and every circumstance.

God Infinitely Concerned

Is the Creator and Preserver of the world unconcerned in what He sees? Does He look upon these things with a malignant or heedless eye? Does He sit at ease in heaven without regarding the poor inhabitants of earth? It cannot be. He has made us, not we ourselves. And He cannot despise the work of His own hands. We are His children, and can a mother forget the children of her womb? She may, yet will not God forget us. He is concerned every moment for what befalls every crea-ture upon earth, and more especially for everything that befalls any of His children. It is hard indeed to comprehend this, but we must believe it unless we will make God a liar.

He is infinite in wisdom as well as in power, and all His wisdom is continually employed in managing the affairs of His creation for the good of His creatures. However, He cannot contradict Himself or undo what He has done. He cannot abolish wickedness or destroy the image of Himself in man. And without doing this, He cannot abolish sin and pain out of the world. Were He to do this, it would imply no wisdom at all, but a stroke of omnipotence. The manifold wisdom of God (as well as all His power and goodness) is displayed in governing man as man—capable of choosing either good or evil. Herein appears the depth of the wisdom of God in His adorable providence.

A Particular Providence

One pious writer speaks of a three-fold circle of divine superintending providence. The outermost circle includes all the descendants of Adam, including heathen and Gentiles. "The Lord is loving unto every man, and His mercy is over all His works." Yet, He takes more immediate care of those in a second circle—a smaller one, which includes all Christians who profess to believe Christ and who in some degree honor Him— at least more than the heathen do. God does likewise in some measure honor them. Within the third, innermost circle are contained only the real Christians who worship God not only in form, but in spirit and in truth. It is to these in particular that He says, "Even the very hairs of your head are all numbered."

But some say, in support of a general providence rather than a particular one, that God never deviates from the general laws He has made. But this is inconsistent with the whole tenor of Scripture. If this were true, there never was a miracle. Did the Almighty confine Himself to these general laws when He divided the Red Sea? Or when He caused the sun to stand still?

Admitting that in the common course of nature God does act by general laws, He has never precluded Himself from making exceptions to them whenever He pleases. The Bible teaches that God hears and answers prayer. Every answer to prayer is, properly, a miracle.

We may learn from God's providence to put our whole trust in Him who has never failed those who seek Him. Fear not, therefore; if you truly fear God, you need fear none besides. He will be a strong tower to all that trust in Him. His favorable kindness covers you as a shield.

Allied to this confidence in God is the thankfulness we owe for His kind protection. Let those give thanks whom the Lord delivers from the hands of all their enemies. How can we sufficiently praise Him while we are under His wings?

In the meantime we should take care to walk humbly and closely with our God and seek to have a conscience void of offence towards God and man.

In what melancholy condition are those who do not believe in Providence, or at least not in a particular one! He who says God is far above and who expects no help from Him has little comfort. On the other hand, how unspeakably *happy* is the man who has the Lord for his help—who can say, "I have set the Lord always before me; because He is on my right hand, I shall not be moved."

Part II
From the Journal

Wesley began his published *Journal* on October 14, 1735 and its last entry is October 24, 1790. Between those Octobers lies an amazing record of human achievement. The selections here touch on formative influences and typical encounters in Wesley's ministry.

Going to America

October 1735

My brother Charles Wesley and I took boat for Gravesend in order to embark for Georgia. Our end in leaving our native country was not to avoid want . . . nor to gain the dung or dross of riches or honor, but singly this: to save our souls—to live wholly to the glory of God.

I began to learn German in order to converse with the twenty-six Germans who were on board. On Sunday, the weather being fair and calm, I preached *extempore* and then administered the Lord's Supper to six or seven communicants. Believing that denying ourselves, even in the smallest instances, might . . . be helpful to us, we wholly left off the use of flesh and wine and confined ourselves to vegetable food— chiefly rice and bisquit.

We now began to be a little regular. Our common way of living was this: from four in the morning till five each of us used private prayer. From five to seven we read the Bible together, carefully comparing it . . . with the writings of the earliest ages. At seven we break-fasted. At eight were the public prayers. From nine to twelve I learned German; my brother wrote sermons, and Mr. Ingham instructed the children, At twelve we met to give an account to one another on what we had done since our last meeting. About one o'clock we dined.

The time from dinner to four we spent with each of those whom each of us had taken in charge. At four were the evening prayers, when either the second lesson was explained, or the children were catechised. From five to six we again used private prayer. From six to seven I read in our cabin to two or three of our passengers, and each of my brethren to a few more in theirs. At seven I joined with the Germans in their public service. At eight we met again to exhort and instruct one another. Between nine and ten we went to bed, where neither the roaring of the sea or the motion of the ship could take away the refreshing sleep which God gave us.

In the evening another storm began. In the morning it increased so that they were forced to let the ship drive. I could not but say to myself, "How is it that thou hast no faith?" being still unwilling to die . . . At noon our third storm began. At four it was more violent then before. At seven I went to the Germans. I had long before observed the great seriousness of their behavior; of their humility they had given continual proof. In the midst of their service the sea split the mainsail in pieces, covered the ship, and poured in between the decks. A terrible screaming began among the English. The Germans calmly sang on. I asked one of them afterwards, "Were you not afraid?" He answered, "I thank God, No." I asked, "But were not your women and children afraid?" He replied mildly, "No, our women and children are not afraid to die."

In Georgia

October 1735 to November 1737
At about eight in the morning we first set foot on American ground. . . . I asked Mr. Spangenberg's advice concerning my own conduct. He said, "My brother, I must first ask you one or two questions. Have you the witness within yourself? Does the Spirit of God bear witness with your spirit that you are a child of God?" I was surprised and knew not what to answer. He observed it and asked, "Do you know Jesus Christ?" I paused and said, "I know He is the Saviour of the world." "True," replied he, "but do you know He has saved you?" I answered, "I hope He has died to save me." He only added, "Do you know yourself?" I said, "I do," but I fear they were vain words.

I consulted my friends as to whether God did not call me to return to England. The reason for my coming in the first place was to instruct the Indians, but I had not found or heard of any Indians on the continent of America who had the least desire of being instructed. Besides, there was a probability of doing more service to that unhappy people in England than I could do in Georgia by representing, without fear or favor, to the trustees the real state the colony was in. After deeply considering these things, they were unanimous that I ought to go, but not yet. So I laid the thoughts of it aside for the present, being persuaded that when the time was come, God would "make the way plain before my face."

I again consulted my friends who agreed with me that the time we looked for was now come. In the afternoon, the magistrate published an order requiring all the officers and sentinels to prevent my going out of the province and forbidding any person to assist me so to do. . . . I clearly saw the hour was come for leaving this place, and as soon as evening prayers were over, about eight o'clock, the tide then serving, I shook off the dust of my feet and left Georgia after having preached the Gospel there one year and nearly nine months.

Before Aldersgate

1738
We had a thorough storm, which obliged us to shut all close, the sea breaking over the ship continually. I was at first afraid, but cried to God and was strengthened. . . . My mind was now full of thought, part of which I wrote down as follows: "I went to America to convert the Indians, but oh, who shall convert me? Who is he that will deliver me from this evil heart of mischief? I can talk well and believe myself while no danger is near. But let death look me in the face and my spirit is troubled."

In London. Many reasons I have to bless God . . . for my having been carried to that strange land contrary to all my preceding resolutions. Hereby, I trust He has in some measure "humbled me and proved me, and shown me what was in my heart" (Deut. 8:2).

I was asked to speak at St. John the Evangelist's. I did so on those strong words, "If any man is in Christ, he is a new creature" (2 Cor. 5:17). I was afterwards informed many of the best in the parish were so offended that I was not to preach there any more. . . . I vistited many of my old friends, as well as most of my relations. I find the time is not yet come when I am to be "hated of all men." Oh, may I be prepared for it!

Meeting with Peter Bohler

At the house of Mr. Weinantz, a Dutch merchant, I met Peter Bohler . . . just then landed from Germany. . . . I set out for Oxford with Peter Bohler. . . . We went to Stanton Harcourt; the next day I preached once more at the castle in Oxford to a numerous and serious congregation.

All this time I conversed much with Peter Bohler, but I understood him not, least of all when he said, "My brother, my brother, that philosophy of yours must be purged away."

With regard to my own behavior, I now renewed and wrote down my former resolutions: (1) To use absolute openness and unreserve with all I should converse with. (2) To labor for continual seriousness, not willingly indulging myself in the least levity of behavior or in laughter. (3) To speak no word which does not tend to the glory of God—in particular, not to talk of worldy things. (4) To take no pleasure which does not tend to the glory of God.

I found my brother at Oxford recovering from his pleurisy, and with him Peter Bohler by whom, in the hand of the great God, I was . . . convinced of unbelief, of the want of that faith whereby alone we are saved. Immediately it struck into my mind, "Leave off preaching. How can you preach to others who have not faith yourself?" I asked Bohler whether he thought I should leave it off or not. He answered, "By no means." "But what can I preach?" He said, "Preach faith till you have it, and then, because you have it, you will preach faith."

I asked P. Bohler again whether I ought not to refrain from teaching others. He said, "No, do not hide in the earth the talent God has given you."

I preached at St. Laurence's in the morning and afterwards at St. Katherine Cree's Church. I was enabled to speak strong words at both, and was therefore the less surprised at being informed I was not to preach any more in either of those churches.

I preached in the morning at St. Ann's, Aldersgate, and in the afternoon at Savoy Chapel on free salvation by faith in the blood of Christ. I was quickly apprised that at St. Alban's, likewise, I am to preach no more.

I preached at St. John's, Wapping, at three and at St. Bennett's, Paul's Wharf, in the evening. At these churches, likewise, I am to preach no more.

Monday, Tuesday, and Wednesday I had continual sorrow and heaviness in my heart.

"I Felt My Heart Strangely Warmed"

I think it was about five this morning that I opened my Testament on those words, "There are given unto us exceeding great and precious promises, even that you should be partakers of the divine nature" (2 Peter 1:4). Just as I went out, I opened it again on those words, "Thou art not far from the kingdom of God" (Mark 12:34). In the afternoon I was asked to go to St. Paul's. The anthem was, "Out of the deep have I called unto Thee, O Lord: Lord, hear my voice. Oh, let Thine ears consider well the voice of my complaint."

In the evening I went very unwillingly to a society in Aldersgate Street, where one was reading Luther's Preface to the Epistle to the Romans. About a quarter before nine, while he was describing the change which God works in the heart through faith in Christ, I felt my heart strangely warmed. I felt I did trust in Christ alone for salvation. And an assurance was given me that He had taken away my sins, even mine, and had saved me from the law of sin and death.

I began to pray with all my might for those who had in a special manner despitefully used me and persecuted me. I then testified openly to all there what I now first felt in my heart. . . . Then was I taught that peace and victory over sin are essential to faith in the Captain of our salvation.

After my return home I was much buffeted with temptations, but I cried out and they fled away. Herein I found the difference between this and my former state. Before I was striving, yea, fighting with all my might under the law, as well as under grace. Then I was sometimes, if not often, conquered; now I was always conqueror.

Yet the enemy injected a fear, "If thou dost believe, why is there not a more sensible change?" I answered, "That I know not. But this I know. I have now peace with God. And I sin not today, and Jesus my Master, has forbidden me to take anxious thought for tomorrow.

Field Preaching

1739
During my stay in London I was fully employed between our own society in Fetter Lane and many others where I was continually asked to expound. I had no thought of leaving London, when I received . . . a letter from Mr. Whitefield and another from Mr. Seward entreating me in the most pressing manner to come to Bristol without delay. This I was not at all forward to do.

I left London and in the evening expounded to a small company at Basingstoke. In the evening I reached Bristol and met Mr. Whitefield. I could scarcely reconcile myself at first to this strange way of preaching in the fields. I had been all my life (till very lately) so tenacious of every point relating to decency and order that I should have thought the saving of souls almost a sin if it had not been done in church.

In the evening (Mr. Whitefield being gone) I began expounding our Lord's Sermon on the Mount . . . to a little society which was accustomed to meet once or twice a week in Nicholas Street. . . . At four in the afternoon I submitted to be more vile and proclaimed in the highways the glad tidings of salvation; speaking from a little eminence in a ground adjoining the city, to about three thousand people. . . . At seven in the morning I preached to about a thousand persons at Bristol, and afterwards to about fifteen hundred on the top of Harmam Mount in Kingswood. I called to them in the words of the evangelical prophet, "Ho, everyone that thirsteth, Come ye to the waters . . . Come and buy wine and milk without money and without price" (Isa. 55:1).

The First Methodist Building

1739
We took possession of a piece of ground near St. James's churchyard in the Horse Fair, Bristol, where it was designed to build a room large enough to contain both societies of Nicholas and Baldwin Street. On Saturday 12, the first stone was laid, with praise.

I had not at first the least apprehension or design of being personally engaged either in the expense of this work or in the direction of it, having appointed eleven feoffees [a person to whom land is given is a fief] on whom I supposed these burdens would fall. But I quickly found my mistake. First, with regard to the expense, the whole undertaking would have stood still had not I immediately taken upon myself the payment of all the workmen so that before I knew where was, I had contracted a debt of more than a hundred and fifty pounds. This I was to discharge as I could, the subscriptions of both societies not amounting to one quarter of the sum.

As to the direction of the work, I presently received letters from my friends in London, Mr. Whitefield in particular . . . that neither he nor they would have anything to do with the building, nor contribute anything towards it, unless I would instantly discharge all feoffees and do everything in my own name. Many reasons they gave for this, but one was enough: such feoffees would always have it in their power to control me, and if I did not preach as they liked, to turn me out of the room I had built.

I accordingly yielded to their advice . . . and took the whole management into my own hands. Money, it is true, I had not, nor any human prospect or probability of procuring it, but I knew "the earth is the Lord's and the fullness thereof," and in His name I set out, nothing doubting.

A Strange Encounter

1740—42

I had designed this morning to set out for Bristol but was unexpectedly prevented. In the afternoon I received a letter from Leicestershire pressing me to come without delay and pay the last office of friendship to one whose soul was on the wing for eternity. I set out.

The next afternoon I stopped at Newport-Pagnell and then rode on till I overtook a serious man, with whom I immediately fell in conversation.

He presently let me know what his opinions were; hence I said nothing to contradict them. But he asked whether I held the same doctrine as he did. I told him repeatedly he had better keep to practical things, lest we be angry with one another.

And so we did for two miles, till he caught me unawares and dragged me into a dispute. He then grew warmer and warmer and told me I was rotten at heart and supposed I was one of John Wesley's followers. I told him, "No, I am John Wesley." Thereupon he would gladly have run away, but being the better mounted of the two, I kept close to his side and endeavored to show him his heart till we came to the street of Northampton.

Preaching on His Father's Tombstone

1740—42

It being many years since I had been at Epworth, I went to an inn in the center of town, not knowing whether any were left who would not be ashamed of my acquaintance. But an old servant of my father's, with two or three poor women, presently found me.

A little before the service began I went to Mr. Romley, the curate, and offered to assist him either by preaching or reading prayers. But he did not care to accept my assistance.

The church was exceedingly full in the afternoon when a rumor was spread that I was to preach. But the sermon on "Quench not the Spirit" (1 Thes. 5:19) was not suitable to the expectation of many of the hearers.

Mr. Romley told them one of the most dangerous ways of quenching the Spirit was by enthusiasm. He enlarged on the character of an enthusiast in a very florid and oratorical manner.

After the sermon, John Taylor stood in the churchyard and gave notice as the people were coming out, "Mr. Wesley, not being permitted to preach in the church, designs to preach at six o'clock."

Accordingly, at six I came and found such a congregation as I believe Epworth never saw before. I stood near the east end of the church, upon my father's tombstone, and cried, "The kingdom of heaven is not meat and drink, but righteousness and peace and joy in the Holy Ghost" (Rom. 14:17).

Death of Wesley's Mother

1740—42

I left Bristol in the evening of Sunday, July 18, and on Tuesday came to London. I found my mother on the borders of eternity, but she had no doubt or fear nor any desire but (as soon as God should call) "to depart and be with Christ."

About three in the afternoon on Friday I went to my mother and found her change was near. I sat down on the bedside. She was in her last conflict, unable to speak, but I believe quite sensible. Her look was calm and serene, and her eyes fixed upward while we commended her soul to God.

From three to four the silver cord was loosing, and the wheel breaking at the cistern. Then, without any struggle or sigh or groan, the soul was set at liberty. We stood around the bed and fulfilled her last request uttered a little while before she lost her speech,

"Children, as soon as I am released, sing a psalm of praise to God."

An innumerable company of people being gathered about five in the afternoon, I committed to the earth the body of my mother to sleep with her fathers. The portion of Scripture from which I afterwards spoke was: "I saw a great white throne . . . And I saw the dead, small and great, stand before God; and the books were opened (Rev. 20:11-12). It was one of the most solemn assemblies I ever saw or expect to see on this side of eternity.

Wesley's Marriage and the Itinerant Preacher

1751

For many years I remained single because I believed I could be more useful in a single than in a married state. And I praise God who enabled me to do so. I now as fully believed that in my present circumstances I might be more useful in a married state. Upon this clear conviction and by the advice of my friends I entered matrimony a few days later.

After preaching at five, I hastened to take my leave of the congregation at Snowfields, purposing to set out in the morning for the north. When on the middle of London Bridge, both my feet slipped on the ice, and I fell with a great force, the bone of my ankle lighting on the top of a stone. However, I got on, with some help, to the chapel, being resolved not to disappoint the people. After preaching, I had my leg bound up by a surgeon and made a shift to walk to the Seven Dials. It was with much difficulty that I got up into the pulpit, but God comforted many of our hearts.

I was carried to the Foundry and preached, kneeling

(as I could not stand), on part of the twenty-third Psalm. My heart was enlarged and my mouth opened to declare the wonders of God's love.

It was the second day I had appointed for my journey, but I was disappointed again, not being yet able to set my foot on the ground. However I preached (kneeling) on Tuesday evening and Wednesday morning.

Being tolerably able to ride, though not to walk, I set out for Bristol. I came there on Wednesday, thoroughly tired, though in some respects better than when I set out.

Having finished the business for which I came to Bristol, I set out again for London. I came to London on Thursday, and having settled all affairs, left it again on Wednesday 27. I cannot understand how a Methodist preacher can, under God, preach one sermon or travel one day less in a married state than in a single state. In this respect surely, "it remaineth that they who have wives be as though they had none."

Wesley's Abounding Vitality

1751—53

While I was preaching at West Street in the afternoon, there was one of the most violent storms I ever remember. In the midst of the sermon a great part of the house opposite the chapel blew down.

I walked over to Burnham. I had no thought of preaching there, doubting if my strength would allow me to preach always three times a day, as I had done most days since I came from Evesham. But finding the house full of people, I could not refrain. Still the more I use my strength, the more I have. I am often much tired the first time I preach in a day; a little the second time; but after the third or fourth, I rarely feel either weakness or weariness.

We rode to Durham, and thence through very rough roads, and as rough weather, to Barnard Castle. I was exceedingly faint when we came in. However, the time having arrived, I went into the street and would have preached, but the mob was so numerous and so loud that it was not possible for many to hear. Nevertheless, I spoke on, and those who were near me listened with great attention. To prevent this, some of the rabble fetched the engine and threw a good deal of water on the congregation, but not a drop fell on me. After about three quarters of an hour, I returned into the house.

My lodging was not such as I would have chosen; but what Providence chooses is always good. My bed was considerably underground, the room serving both for a bedchamber and cellar. The closeness was more troublesome at first than the coolness, but I let in a little fresh air by breaking a pane of paper (put in place of glass) in the window and then slept soundly till the morning.

Wesley at Eighty-Five

June 28, 1788
In the conclusion of the morning service we had a remarkable service and the same in the evening, moving the whole congregation as the heart of one man.

This day I enter on my eighty-sixth year. I now find I grow old: (1) my sight is decayed so I cannot read small print unless in a strong light. (2) My strength is decayed so that I walk much more slowly than I did some years since. (3) My memory of names, whether of persons or places, is decayed till I stop a little to recollect them. What I should be afraid of if I took thought for the tomorrow is that my body should weigh down my mind and create either stubbornness by the decrease of my understanding or peevishness by the increase of bodily infirmities. But Thou shalt answer for me, O Lord My God.

January 1, 1790

I am now an old man, decayed from head to foot. My eyes are dim, my right hand shakes much, my mouth is hot and dry every morning. I have a lingering fever almost every day. My motion is weak and slow. However, blessed be God, I do not slack my labor. I can preach and write still.

Wesley's Last Hours
(By one who was present)

Saturday, February 26, 1791. He continued much the same, spoke but little and only if roused.

Monday, February 28. His weakness increased apace. . . . Dr. Whitehead desired they should call in another physician, but Wesley refused. He slept most of the day, spoke but little. . . . Once in a low but distinct manner he said, "There is no way into the holiest but by the blood of Jesus."

Thursday, March 1. He never complained through his whole illness, except once when he said he felt a pain in his left breast when he drew his breath. He began singing,

> All glory to God in the sky,
> And peace upon earth be restor'd

Having sung two verses, his strength failed. He called on Mr. Bradford to give him a pen and ink, but his right hand had forgot its cunning. I said, "Let me write for you. Tell me what you would say." "Nothing," returned he, "but that God is with us."

When he got into his chair, we saw him change for death. Regardless of his dying frame he said with a weak voice, "Lord, Thou givest strength to those that can speak and to those that cannot . . ." His voice failed, and after grasping for breath he said, "Now we have done; let us go." We were obliged to lay him down on the bed from which he rose no more. But after lying still and sleeping a little, he called me to him and said, "Betsy, you, Mr. Bradford, and the others pray and praise." We knelt down and truly our hearts were filled with the Divine Presence; the room seemed to be filled with God.

Though he strove to speak we could not understand his words. After a pause he summoned all his strength and cried out, "The best of all, God is with us."

PART III

Wesley's Select Letters
Chiefly about
the Christian Faith

Select Letters

What Is a Christian?
To His Brother Samuel, London, October 30, 1738
With regard to my own character and doctrine, I shall answer you very plainly. By a Christian, I mean one who so believes in Christ that sin has no more dominion over him. In this obvious sense of the word, I was not a Christian till May 24th past. For till then sin had the dominion over me, although I fought with it continually. But surely, then, from that time to this, it has not; such is the free grace of God in Christ. What sins they were which, till then, reigned over me, and from which, by the grace of God, I am now free, I am ready to declare on the housetop, if it may be for the glory of God.

O brother, would to God you would leave disputing concerning the things which you know not (if indeed you know them not) and beg of God to fill up what is yet wanting in you.

Wesley Demurs Against Legalism
To The Rev. William Law May 14, 1738
Reverend Sir:

It is in obedience to what I think to be the call of God that I, who have the sentence of death in my own soul, take upon me to write to you, of whom I have often desired to learn the first elements of the Gospel of Christ.

If you are born of God you will approve of the design, though it be but weakly executed. If not, I shall grieve for you, not for myself. For as I seek not the praise of men, so neither regard I the contempt either of you or any other.

For two years . . . I have been preaching after the model of your two practical treatises [*Christian Perfection and A Serious Call to a Devout and Holy Life*]. All that heard have allowed that the law is great, wonderful, and holy. But no sooner did they attempt to fulfill it but they found it too high for man, and that by doing "the works of the law shall no flesh be justified."

To remedy this, I exhorted them . . . to pray earnestly for the grace of God, and to use all the other means of obtaining that grace which the all-wise God has appointed. But still, both they and I were more and more convinced that this is a law by which a man cannot live, the law in our members continually warring against it and bringing us into deeper captivity to the law of sin.

Under this heavy yoke I might have groaned till death, had not a holy man, to whom God lately directed me, upon my complaining thereof, answered at once, "Believe and thou shalt be saved. Believe in the Lord Jesus Christ with all thy heart, and nothing shall be impossible to thee."

I beseech you, sir, by the mercies of God, to consider deeply and impartially whether the true reason of your never pressing this upon me was that you had it not yourself? . . . Let me beg you to consider whether your extreme roughness and morose and sour behavior, at least on many occasions, can possibly be the fruit of a living faith in Christ?

Wesley Acknowledges Moravian Piety

To the Church of God which is in Hernhutt. October 14, 1738
Glory be to God, even the Father of our Lord Jesus Christ, for His unspeakable gift—for giving me to be

an eye-witness of your faith, and love, and holy conversation in Christ Jesus! I have borne testimony thereof with all plainness of speech in many parts of Germany.

We are endeavoring here also . . . to be followers of you, as you are of Christ. Fourteen were added to us since our return, so that we now have eight bands of men, consisting of fifty-six persons, all of whom seek for salvation only in the blood of Christ. As yet we have only two small bands of women. . . . But here are many others who only wait till we have leisure to instruct them.

Though my brother and I are not permitted to preach in most of the churches in London, yet (thanks be to God!) there are others left wherein we have liberty to speak the truth. . . . Every evening and on set evenings in the week at two places, we publish the word of reconciliation, sometimes to twenty or thirty, sometimes to fifty or sixty, sometimes to three or four hundred persons.

O cease not, ye that are highly favored, to beseech our Lord that He would be with us even to the end.

On Sanctification

To Miss Furly, Afterward Mrs. Downes. December 22, 1756
My Dear Sister:

Whereunto you have attained, hold fast. But expect that greater things are at hand, although our friend talks as if you were not to expect them till the article of death.

Certainly sanctification (in the proper sense) is "an instantaneous deliverance from all sin" and includes "an instantaneous power then given always to cleave to

God." Yet this sanctification (at least in the lower degree) does not include a power never to think a useless thought nor ever to speak a useless word. I myself believe that such a perfection is inconsistent with living in a corruptible body, for this makes it impossible "always to think right." While we breathe, we shall, more or less, make mistakes. If, therefore, Christian perfection implies otherwise, we must not expect it till after death.

I want you to be all love. This is the perfection I believe and teach. And this perfection is consistent with a thousand nervous disorders, which that high-strained perfection is not. Indeed, my judgment is that to overdo is to undo; and that to set perfection too high is the most effectual way of driving it out of the world.

Christian Perfection Explained

To Miss H———, Dublin, April 5, 1758

"The doctrine of perfection," you say, has perplexed you much, "since some of our preachers have placed it in so dreadful a light, one of them affirming, 'a believer, till perfect, is under the curse of God,' and another 'If you die before you have attained it, you will surely perish.'"

By *perfection*, I mean, *perfect love* or the loving God with all our heart, so as to rejoice evermore, to pray without ceasing, and in everything to give thanks. I am convinced every believer may attain this. Yet, I do not say he is in a state of damnation or under the curse of God till he does attain. No, he is in a state of grace and in favor with God as long as he believes. Neither would I say, "If you die without it, you will perish," but rather, "till you are saved from unholy tempers you are not ripe for glory."

"But none can attain perfection unless they first believe it attainable." Neither do I affirm this. I know a Calvinist in London who never believed it attainable till the moment she did attain it, and then she lay declaring it aloud for many days till her spirit returned to God.

Guide to Family Living

[*The following letter was written to Mr. Wesley's housekeeper at Bristol*]

To Mrs. Sarah Ryan. Newbury, November 8, 1757

My Dear Sister:

In the hurry of business I had not time to write down what you desired—the rules of our family. So I snatch a few minutes to do it now, and the more cheerfully because I know you will observe them.

1. The family rises, part at four, part at four-thirty.
2. They breakfast at seven, dine at twelve, and sup at six.
3. They spend the hour from five to six in the evening (after a little joint prayer) in private.
4. They pray together at nine, and then retire to their chambers, so that all are in bed before ten.
5. They observe all Fridays in the year as days of fasting or abstinence.

You in particular I advise: suffer no impertinent visitor, no unprofitable conversation in the house. It is a city set upon a hill, and all that is in it should be "holiness to the Lord."

On what a pinnacle do you stand! You are placed in the eye of all the world, friends, and enemies. You have no experience of these things, no knowledge of the people, no advantages of education, nor large natural abilities, and are but a novice, as it were, in the ways of

God. It requires all the omnipotent love of God to preserve you in your present station.

Stand fast in the Lord, and in the power of His might. Show that nothing is too hard for Him. Take to thee the whole armor of God. Do and suffer all things through Christ strengthening you. If you continue teachable and advisable, I know nothing that shall be able to hurt you.

Wesley Reproves a Young Minister

To Mr. John Trembath, Tiverton, September 21, 1755
The plain reason why I did not design to speak with you at Launceston was that I had no hope of doing you good. I observed long ago that you are not patient of reproof; and I fear you are less so now than ever. But since you desire it, I will tell you once more what I think concerning you.

I think you tasted of the powers of the world to come thirteen or fourteen years ago and were then simple of heart and willing to spend and be spent for Christ. But not long after, not being sufficiently on your guard, you suffered loss by being applauded. This revived and increased your natural vanity, which was the harder to be checked because of your innate stubbornness.

O remember from whence you have fallen! Repent and do the first works! First, recover the life of God in your own soul and walk as Christ walked. Walk with God as you did twelve years ago. Then you might again be useful to His children.

Wesley Reproves for Pride and Enthusiasm

To Mrs. R———, Whitehaven, June 28, 1766
My Dear Sister:
For some time I have been convinced it was my duty

to tell you what was on my mind. I will do it with all plainness. You may answer this letter or not, as you judge best.

Many things I have observed in you which gave me pleasure, some which gave me concern. The former I need not mention; the latter I must, or I should not myself be clear before God.

The first of these is something that looks like pride. You sometimes seem to think too highly of yourself, and to despise others. I shall mention two or three particulars:

1. You appear to be above instruction.

2. You appear to think that none understands the doctrine of sanctification like you. I know several, both men and women, who both think and speak so scripturally of it as you do, and perhaps more clearly. There is something dark and confused in your manner of speaking concerning it.

3. You appear to undervalue the experience of almost everyone in comparison to your own.

Another thing which gives me concern is, I am afraid you are in danger of enthusiasm. We know there are dreams and impressions but how easily you may be deceived herein! How easily we mix something from God with something from nature, especially if we have a lively imagination.

I will mention one thing more. It has frequently been said that you endeavor to monopolize the affections of all that fall into your hands—that you destroy the nearest and dearest connection that they had before and make them quite cool and indifferent to their most intimate friends.

I commend you to God and to the Word of His grace.

Warnings Against Slackness

To a Member of the Society. May 31, 1762
Dear———:

Is your mind always stayed on God? Do you find every thought brought into captivity to the obedience of Christ? Do not vain thoughts (useless, trifling, unedifying) lodge within you? Does not the corruptible body at times press down the soul? Has God made your very dreams devout? I have known Satan to assault during sleep those whom he could not touch when they were awake.

As to your band, there are two sorts of persons with whom you may have to do—the earnest and the slack. You must deal with each differently. The latter you must search and find out why they are slack and exhort them to repent, to be zealous, and do the first works. The former you have only to encourage, to exhort, to push forward to the mark, to bid them grasp the prize so high.

Believe more, love more; you cannot love enough. Beware of sins of omission.

Remedy for Satan's Assault

To a Member of the Society. July 13, 1771
Dear ———:

As long as we dwell in a house of clay it is liable to affect the mind—sometimes by dulling or darkening the understanding, and sometimes more directly by damping and depressing the soul. In this state, doubt or fear of one kind or another will naturally arise. And the prince of this world, who knows whereof we are made, will not fail to improve the occasion to disturb, though he cannot pollute the heart which God has cleansed from all unrighteousness.

In the thirteenth chapter of 1 Corinthians you have the height and depth of perfection. St. Paul speaks of the love of our neighbor as flowing from the deep love of God. . . . That darkness which often clouds your understanding, I take to be quite preternatural. I believe the spirit of darkness spreads a mist over your mind so far as he is permitted, and that the best remedy is simply to look up to God and the cloud will flee away at His presence.

Improving the Mind

To a Member of the Society. July 1, 1772

Dear———:

It is lost time to consider whether you write well or ill: you speak from the heart, and that is enough. Unbelief is either total, the absence of faith, or partial, the want of more faith. In the latter sense every believer may complain of unbelief, unless when he is filled with faith and the Holy Ghost. Then it is all midday. Yet even then we may pray, "Lord, increase our faith."

We learn to think by reading and meditating on what we read, by conversing with sensible people, and by everything that improves the heart. Since purity of heart both clears the medium through which we see and strengthens the faculty, mechanical rules avail little, unless one had opportunity of learning the elements of logic; but it is a miserable task to learn them without an instructor.

Entire resignation implies entire love. Give Him your will, and you give Him your heart.

You need not be at all careful in that matter, whether you apply directly to one person or the other, seeing He and the Father are one. Pray just as you are led, without reasoning, in all simplicity. Be a little child, hanging on Him that loves you.

Always in Haste . . . Never in a Hurry

To a Member of the Society

Dear————:

You do not understand my manner of life. Though I am always in haste, I am never in a hurry, because I never undertake any more work than I can go through with perfect calmness of spirit. It is true I travel four or five thousand miles in a year. But I generally travel alone in my carriage; and, consequently, am as retired ten hours in a day as if I was in a wilderness. On other days I never spend less than three hours (frequently ten or twelve) in the day alone. So there are few persons in the kingdom who spend so many hours secluded from all company. Yet I find time to visit the sick and the poor; and I must do it, if I believe the Bible, if I believe these are the marks whereby the Shepherd of Israel will know and judge His sheep at the great day: therefore, when there is time and opportunity for it, who can doubt but this is matter of absolute duty? When I was at Oxford, and lived almost like a hermit, I saw not how any busy man could be saved. I scarce thought it possible for a man to retain the Christian spirit amid the noise and bustle of the world. God taught me better by my own experience. I had ten times more business in America than ever. before in my life. But it was no hindrance to my silence of spirit.

Mr. Boehm was chaplain to Prince George of Denmark, secretary to him and Queen Anne, principal manager of almost all the public charities in the kingdom, and employed in numberless private charities. An intimate friend, knowing this, said to him when they were alone, "Sir, are you not hurt by that amazing hurry of business? I have seen you in your office, surrounded with people, listening to one, dictating to another, and at the same time writing to a third. Could you then retain a sense of the presence of God?" He answered, "All that company, and all that business, no more hindered or lessened my communion with God, than if I had been all alone in a church kneeling before the communion table."

In Defense of Holy Living

To The Rev. Mr. F———. St. Ives, September 15, 1762

Dear Sir:

I have entirely lost my taste for controversy. I have lost my readiness in disputing; and I take this to be a providential discharge from it. All I can now do with a clear conscience is, not to enter into a formal controversy about the new birth, or justification by faith, any more than Christian perfection, but simply to declare my judgment, and to explain myself as clearly as I can, upon any difficulty that may arise concerning it.

So far I can go with you, but no farther. I still say, and without any self-contradiction, I know no persons living who are so deeply conscious of their needing Christ, both as Prophet, Priest, and King, as those who believe themselves, and whom I believe, to be cleansed from all sin; I mean, from all pride, anger, evil desire, idolatry, and unbelief. These very persons feel more than ever their own ignorance, littleness of grace, coming short of the full mind that was in Christ, and walking less accurately than they might have done after their divine Pattern. They are more convinced of the insufficiency of all they are, have, or do, to bear the eye of God without a mediator, and are more penetrated with the sense of the want of Him than ever they were before.

Holiness By Faith

To Lady———. London, June 19, 1771
My Dear Lady:

Many years since I saw that "without holiness no man shall see Lord." I began following after it, and inciting all with whom I had any intercourse to do the same. Ten years after, God gave me a clearer view than I had before of the way how to attain this; namely, by faith in the Son of God. And immediately I declared to all, "We are saved from sin, we are made holy, by faith." This I testified in private, in public, in print; and God confirmed it by a thousand witnesses. I have continued to declare this for above thirty years; and God hath continued to confirm the word of His grace. But during this time well nigh all the religious world hath set themselves in array against me, and, among the rest, many of my own children, following the example of one of my eldest sons, Mr. W———. Their general cry has been, "He is unsound in the faith; he preaches another gospel!" I answer, whether it be the same which they preach or not, it is the same which I have preached for above thirty years. This may easily appear from what I have published during that term.

Encouragement in Temptation

To Miss Jane Hilton, Afterward Mrs. Barton of Beverly. Guiseley, July 1, 1768
My Dear Sister:

You must now expect temptations. Perhaps they

will assault you on every side; for all the powers of hell are enraged at you, and will use every art to move you from your steadfastness. But He that is for you is greater than all that are against you: only beware of evil reasoning! Hang simply on Him that loves you, and whom you love; just as a little helpless child. Christ is yours, all yours: that is enough. Lean your whole soul upon Him! Do you find a witness in yourself that He has cleansed your heart? Do you feel this always? And have you a constant sense of the loving presence of God? You never need lose anything that God has given, so you keep close to Him. Be little and mean in your own eyes, glorying only in the Lord. And do not cease to pray for

Your affectionate brother,

Go from House to House
To a Young Disciple. London, January 8, 1774
Dear Joseph:

Many persons are in danger of reading too little: you are in danger of reading too much. Wherever you are, take up your cross and visit all the society from house to house. Do this according to Mr. Baxter's plan laid down in the Minutes of the Conference. The fruit which will ensue (perhaps in a short time) will abundantly reward your labour. Fruit also we shall have, even in those who have no outward connection with us.

I am glad you "press all believers" to aspire after the full liberty of the children of God. They must not give up their faith in order to do this: herein you formerly seemed to be in some mistake. Let them go on from faith to faith; from weak faith to that strong faith which not only conquers but casts out sin. Meantime it is certain, many call themselves believers who do not even conquer sin, who are strangers to the whole inward kingdom of God, and who are void of the whole fruit of the Spirit.

Guide to Personal Reading

To a Young Disciple. January 25, 1771

As you desire a few directions with regard to the improvement of your mind, I will set down just what occurs to me at present. Only as my business is great, and my time is short, I cannot stay to explain them at large.

All the knowledge you want is comprised in one book—the Bible. When you understand this, you will know enough. I advise you, therefore, to begin every day (before and after private prayer) with reading a portion, more or less, of the Old or New Testament, or of both, if you have time, together with the Notes, which may lead you by the hand into suitable meditation. After breakfast, you may read, in order, the volumes of Sermons, and the other practical books with meditation and prayer. Young, Milton, and the Moral and Sacred Poems, you may read chiefly in the afternoons. Whatever you write, you should write in the forenoons. Take care never to read or write too long at a time. That is not conducive either to bodily or spiritual health. If I can be of use to you in anything else, tell me: you know you may speak freely to me.

Yours affectionately.

Selected Bibliography

Primary Sources
The following are basic to any serious study of Wesley:

The Journal of The Rev. John Wesley. E. Nehemiah Curnock. The Standard Edition. Eight vols. London, 1938.

The Letters of The Rev. John Wesley. Ed. John Telford. The Standard Edition. Eight vols. London, 1931.

The Sermons of John Wesley. Ed. E.H. Sugden. The Standard Edition. Four vols. London, 1921.

Secondary Sources
There is an immense literature about Wesley and the rise of Methodism. The following suggest a few helpful sources:

Baker, Eric. *A Herald of the Evangelical Revival.* London, 1948. A critical inquiry into the relation of William Law to John Wesley and the beginnings of Methodism.

Carter, Henry. *The Methodist Heritage,* New York, 1951. A helpful general picture of the Wesleyan theological heritage.

Fitchett, W.H. *Wesley and His Century*. New York, 1906. Useful for a review of the cross-currents of the eighteenth century.

Lecky, William E. *A History of England in Eighteenth-Century*. Seven vols. London, 1892.

Turner, George A. *A More Excellent Way*. Winona Lake, 1952. A thorough analysis of the heart of John Wesley's message.